LEGAL WRITING

Legal Writing guides students comprehensively through this vital legal skill and addresses a range of assessment methods from exam questions to final essays and problem answers. It considers how to deconstruct essay and problem questions and how to conduct and apply legal research to answer set questions.

Lisa Webley explains how to reference others' work clearly and correctly, making this book a useful tool for students concerned about issues of plagiarism. It also focuses on how to develop critical thinking and communicate legal arguments, with both good and bad examples of written work considered and discussed in the text.

Legal Writing is particularly useful for undergraduate students, especially at the beginning of degree studies, and for GDL and CPE students too.

This fully revised fourth edition includes:

- Guidance on the avoidance of plagiarism including examples of poor practice and best practice.
- Worked examples throughout the text, including guidance on deciphering essay questions in exams and coursework, along with additional examples from across the legal curriculum on the companion website.
- An improved companion website with increased guidance for revision to allow students to test their progress and further engage with the topics in the book.

Clearly written and easy to use, *Legal Writing* enables students to fully engage with essay and exam writing as a vital foundation to their undergraduate degree.

www.routledge.com/cw/webley

Dr Lisa Webley is Professor of Empirical Legal Studies at the University of Westminster and a Senior Fellow at the Institute of Advanced Legal Studies. She teaches on undergraduate and postgraduate courses, including constitutional and administrative law, family law, legal skills, the English legal system and research methods. She is a Senior Fellow of the Higher Education Academy and a Fellow of the Royal Society of Arts.

LEGAL WRITING

fourth edition

LISA WEBLEY

Routledge
Taylor & Francis Group

LONDON AND NEW YORK

Fourth edition published 2016
by Routledge
2 Park Square, Milton Park, Abingdon, Oxon OX14 4RN

and by Routledge
711 Third Avenue, New York, NY 10017

Routledge is an imprint of the Taylor & Francis Group, an informa business

© 2016 Lisa Webley

The right of Lisa Webley to be identified as author of this work has been asserted by her in accordance with sections 77 and 78 of the Copyright, Designs and Patents Act 1988.

First edition published by Cavendish Publishing 2005
Third edition published by Routledge 2013

British Library Cataloguing in Publication Data
A catalogue record for this book is available from the British Library

Library of Congress Cataloging-in-Publication Data
A catalog record for this title has been requested

ISBN: 978-1-138-84110-9 (hbk)
ISBN: 978-1-138-84068-3 (pbk)
ISBN: 978-1-315-73244-2 (ebk)

Typeset in Adobe Garamond
by Wearset Ltd, Boldon, Tyne and Wear

MIX
Paper from
responsible sources
FSC
www.fsc.org   FSC® C013056

Printed and bound in Great Britain by
TJ International Ltd, Padstow, Cornwall

CONTENTS

ACKNOWLEDGEMENTS

I should like to thank, as ever, my parents Jan and Paul Webley and my sister Jemma for their continual patience. I am very grateful for the support of my friends Ruth Baxter, Sarah Turnbull and Bruce Butcher, and for my friends and colleagues at work, including Liz Duff and particularly Steve Greenfield, with whom I taught legal skills for many years. I have learnt a lot from many of the LLB students at the University of Westminster; many have provided valuable feedback on previous editions. I should also like to thank the Law School for allowing me to make use of adapted versions of some of the materials that Steve Greenfield and I first developed and used on the Legal Skills and Process 1 first-year module some years ago. Finally, I should like to thank the anonymous and not so anonymous reviewers who commented on the first, second and third editions of this book and provided useful guidance on how to improve it. Given space constraints in the book, I have incorporated many of the suggestions on the companion website. As ever, all omissions and errors in the book are entirely mine. The book remains a work in progress and, in the spirit of legal writing, I should be happy to receive feedback on how it may be improved in the future.

Lisa Webley
London
August 2015

AN INTRODUCTION TO LEGAL WRITING

Law degrees involve a lot of written work. Lecturers stress that the manipulation and use of language are at the heart of the common law legal tradition. Students are expected to be able to write in a range of styles, to a high standard; they are reminded that effective communication is the key to success, as is their use of evidence and argument. And yet law degrees in the UK, in contrast to their US cousins, rarely focus on writing skills. Traditionally, many academics have expected students to arrive at university with well-formed writing skills, believing that these will have been taught previously at A2 stage and Access Course stage. We are beginning to recognise that this is not always the case. In any event, we can always improve on our written abilities. Writing skills are not things that you learn once and then continue to put into practice in the same way, year after year. Further, writing is one means through which we learn what we think. It is an integral part of our thought process and not simply a means to an end, i.e. to communicate what we think. We could all benefit from tips, good practice suggestions and examples of how our writing could be improved. I hope that this book will provide some of those to help you on your writing journey.

Legal writing is something that many of us will do every day, but we rarely receive feedback on our written style unless our work is being formally assessed either by a lecturer or, in the case of an academic, by another academic who is reviewing our work for potential publication. On that basis, in order to improve we need to develop reflexive skills so that we can critique our own work and learn to develop on our own. We also need to maximise the learning opportunity from the few occasions when we do get informal and formal feedback from others on our writing.

Many of you will be reading this book because you have been set an assessment to do and you are looking for help or a means to improve your marks. Students often tell lecturers that they find the way they are assessed a complete mystery. They explain that they write an essay or an answer to a problem question, but do not really understand what they are supposed to do, how to go about it and what the marks they are awarded really mean about the quality of their answer. It is all just too confusing. A number of factors contribute to a good written answer and we shall address the important ones as we work our way through the book. They include the extent to which the student has:

- understood the task that has been set;

- understood how they will be assessed;

- carried out research of the relevant law;

- taken appropriate notes on relevant legal and related issues;

- identified issues that are relevant to answering the question;

- planned the answer;

- written and presented the issues to answer the question;

- provided evidence in support of the points being made;

- referenced others' work; and

- polished the final draft.

It all sounds terribly hard work and rather complicated. Having said that, some of these stages come naturally to each one of us and the others can be learnt. This book will take you through each one in turn to help you to improve your written work in law.

Most law students will be asked to write two main types of written work: essay answers and problem question answers. There are other forms of written assessment including reflective essays (which also follow similar patterns to standard essays but require the student to reflect on their own performance, their skills and knowledge), and memos and briefing sheets (not dissimilar to problem question answers). Students may also research and write an extended essay or dissertation at some point in their undergraduate or postgraduate studies. Dissertations are essays that include a greater research component, but are more similar to essays in written style than to problem question answers.

Despite the differences between these forms of written work, there are some easy basic rules that work for most forms of written assessment. Writing an essay or giving an answer to a problem question is simply a way to communicate what you think about the issues raised in the title or the scenario in the problem. Written answers such as these demonstrate the weight of evidence that you have in favour of each of the propositions that you raise – in other words the authority of your opinion. The arguments that you make and the evidence that you present feed into the conclusions that you reach. Assessments may feel like impossible feats, but they are really relatively easy as long as you follow a few easy steps and – and this is the hard part – you start to write more than 24 hours before your deadline and you comply with the assessment requirements!

Excellent written work is a culmination of a number of factors coming together. It is a product of a good written style that communicates the ideas in the right way to the relevant audience. Excellent written work focuses on the main issues that have been raised by the question or scenario. It does not end at description, but also provides analysis and critique. Your analysis (your authoritative scholarly/legal professional opinion) needs to be justified through your discussion of how the authoritative evidence that you have found through your research backs up what you are saying. It culminates in a well-considered conclusion that sums up the analysis that you have provided, as a final answer to the question. But it does help for the writer to understand what they are trying to communicate, to what end and to whom. Thus strong written work is not simply a means of showing what you have learned through your attendance in class, your reading and your research. It demonstrates how well you can use that knowledge by applying it to a question or a set of facts. It also demonstrates how effectively you marshal and explain your evidence base so as to construct arguments and reach a scholarly or professional opinion. It communicates your analysis clearly and persuades the reader that you have reached a considered and evidenced conclusion. Writing is a means to communicate your position (your analysis) and to persuade the reader that your position is a valid one. It is not simply a means to show what you know, but instead a way of demonstrating what you can do with what you know.

This introductory chapter will explain the purpose of essays, answers to problem questions and dissertations, in the hope that this will set you on the right track. After that you may want to follow through the steps in the order presented. You should end up with a reasonable essay or problem answer, if you do. If in doubt, stick with the formula. But, if you are confident, you may come up with your own; there is no one correct way to go about writing. What follows is simply one view of how to communicate your views effectively; there are others, some of which are discussed in the books listed in the bibliography. You may wish to look at some of those as well to help you. But do assess your own work to examine the extent to which you have answered the question set, you have developed your own analysis (scholarly or professional opinion) based on solid and authoritative evidence, reached a conclusion that is crisp and clearly communicated, and persuaded the reader that your arguments and evidence justify this conclusion. And work your way through some of the additional guidance, examples and exercises on the companion site too.

THE PURPOSE OF AN ESSAY

> An essay question is a way of examining your understanding and your considered and evidenced views on an area of law, practice or policy. Your answer displays your considered response to a question, which weighs up competing viewpoints. It shows how you reached your conclusions with the evidence that you have drawn upon to come to your final view.

Your first response to any essay should be to spend some time considering what the question is asking you to do. Essays are assessed against the question that has been set, not against your general knowledge of the subject area (as shown in the specimen assessment criteria in the next chapter). Your diagnosis of the nature of the question will either send you off on the correct path, or will send you on a wild goose chase. Spend time reading the question and checking that you understand it. Once you are clear on the nature of the question, it is important that you focus on its purpose. Have you been asked to do one of the following things and, if so, are you clear on what that means?

Analyse: This wording causes difficulties for many students, because they are unsure what analysis is. It would perhaps be easier were academics to write, in place of 'analyse', 'provide your own scholarly opinion'. Analysis is that which you have worked out for yourself (your conclusions) having looked at authoritative evidence from all sides. The strength of your analysis is evident through the justifications you provide (your discussion) along with the evidence that you explain in support of your analysis. Consequently, to analyse means to look at the available evidence, to sort it and structure it (often into themes relating to the question) and to reach a scholarly conclusion. Most essay questions will ask for some variation on this theme. Problem questions also expect you to reach an authoritative (professional) opinion having looked at the strengths and weaknesses of the client's case in the light of the relevant case and legislative provisions that pertain to the client's situation. So, you need to locate relevant material, read and understand it, consider it in the light of the question, describe it (summarise it in your own words), then sort it so that all the evidence on a particular theme appears together (this helps with structure) and redraft the material to explain how that evidence when applied to the question helps you to reach your own conclusion on that point.

Contrast: This is sometimes written as 'compare and contrast' and is perhaps easier to understand if you substitute the word 'compare' for contrast. You should consider the similarities and differences between the issues set out in the question and provide evidence to back up what you are saying in your essay. As above you will need to locate relevant material, read and understand it, consider it in the light of the question, describe it (summarise it in your own words) and then focus on the similarities and differences of the different arguments and explain and justify these similarities and differences in the context of the question.

Criticise: Criticise sometimes appears as 'critically assess' or 'critically analyse'. Some questions may use the word '**critique**' instead. Criticise does not mean that you only write about the negative things that you find during your research, or that you give your view on whether you personally agree with the sentiments expressed in the question. It denotes that you should conduct in-depth research and then examine the research evidence that you have found so as to offer a thoughtful and nuanced opinion (critical analysis) by way of con-clusion and within each paragraph. It is really an instruction to you to think critically – to consider the issue in detail and from all sides (and obviously seek out views that contradict your own personal opinions). This is one of the more sophisticated forms of thinking as it requires you to undertake a good deal of research, and to work all the way through description and analysis to weigh up all the evidence that you have found in a sophisticated way and reach nuanced, subtle conclusions on each point you are making.

Discuss and/or do you agree? (often after a quote): The answer to this cannot be just 'yes' or 'no'! Your essay should define the issues in the question and then move on to consider different viewpoints on those issues, or different research evidence on those issues. You may find it helpful to write down the strengths and weaknesses or arguments for and against the proposition men-tioned in the quotation. Make sure that you have cases, law and/or other writers to support these. You should conclude by giving your considered view on the quotation once you have worked your way through others' views and weighed up the evidence.

Evaluate: Give your opinion on the validity of a statement made or an issue raised in the question in the light of evidence you have to support differing view-points from your research/reading. This is similar to a 'discuss' question but with reference to a particular focus indicated in the wording of the question.

Explain: What is the significance of whatever was set out in the question? Give a definition of the issues raised in the question, followed by an outline of the nature of the issues and the implications of the issues. You will need to do some research or have done some research in order to answer this type of question properly. The questioner is unlikely to want you to stop at pure description (reporting on what others say) but instead will usually expect some critique as well.

Examine: This is very similar to discuss, although it implies a little more analysis, including an assessment of merit, whether the question implies that you should be considering positives and negatives, or the extent to which something is working well or is in need of reform. You should take your lead from the question to establish the issue that you are examining and the way in which you are to analyse it.

Outline/summarise: Give the main points in relation to the issue raised in the question, without getting stuck in the detail of the issue. This is similar to providing an overview.

For the most part, all of the instructions set out above are asking you to do some research or reading on the topic in the question, or to have done some before entering the exam room. Such questions aim to test your ability to structure your knowledge and then apply it to the question to provide a considered, persuasive response that takes into account relevant authoritative evidence. An essay may be set to assess your ability to conduct research, to identify and note relevant authoritative evidence as well as to assess your understanding and your writing skills. If this is the case then leave plenty of time within which to complete the main research stage before you begin the writing stage. Chapter 5 provides a brief guide to how to carry out library-based research and how to use your research findings in your writing.

An essay may also have been set to assess your ability to write under timed conditions. If this is the case then you may be expected to carry out research on a given topic prior to the timed essay, to include relevant research findings in a notebook and then to use your research findings under timed conditions to answer a question on the given topic. This type of assessment requires you to conduct your research in detail and to organise your research evidence into a notebook in advance of the day of the timed essay. You may be able to write a good essay under timed conditions, but without the research, the evidence, to back up your points you will not do as well as you would have hoped. You will be expected to provide more evidence in support of your arguments if you are permitted to take materials into an exam room or to write your coursework with access to your notes. It will be important to work out the key issues on the topic or question before you enter the exam room. You may wish to do a detailed plan (see Chapter 4 for help with plans).

In short, an excellent essay provides a complete answer to the question within the confines of the word limit. It is written in good English, in a style that is appropriate to the intended audience. All points made are backed up with authoritative evidence. Finally, the essay meets any assessment requirements.

THE PURPOSE OF A PROBLEM ANSWER

A problem question is a scenario that sets out the facts of a given situation. The facts are there to prompt the writer (usually acting as a barrister) to give a legal opinion to the party or parties, to assist them in deciding what legal action they should take, if any. They are designed to test your legal knowledge and your ability to apply the law to specific facts so as to provide a prediction of the likely outcome and/or possible avenues for negotiation for settlement.

A problem question tests your ability to analyse the facts in the scenario and to work out which ones are agreed or accepted by all the parties (different sides) in the scenario, which ones are disputed and must be discussed and which facts are not discussed but may have a bearing on the outcome of the case. Those facts that are important but are not present in the problem question should be mentioned in the answer so that the solicitor or direct client, the person to whom you are writing your opinion, may investigate those facts further before proceeding with the case.

A problem question also tests your ability to diagnose the legal issues that are relevant to the parties and to provide a considered response on the likely outcome of each point of law, if they were to be argued in court on the basis of the facts as presented. This is done by arguing the competing precedents and statutory points that relate to the facts in the question. You will need to display your understanding of the law in the area by referring to cases and to statutes and other legislation to back up the general principles of law that you explain to the solicitor representing the party to be advised. Dexterous use of case law and legislation should allow you to reach a nuanced understanding of the client's legal position so that you can provide effective legal advice. You will need to employ your understanding of statutory interpretation for UK legislation and also EU law. You will need to become adept at applying and distinguishing helpful and unhelpful precedents, which you will need to read so as to develop your understanding of the *ratio* and its application to the facts in the problem question. To do this you will also need strong research skills so that you are able to find all the relevant authorities. You will also need to be dexterous in your manipulation of law (to argue competing interpretations) and your application of law to the facts. In addition, you will need to persuade the reader that you have reached robust conclusions on each point of law by explaining how the evidence backs up your analysis. You should communicate your analysis clearly and in a logical order such that the reader is able to follow the thread of your arguments and see how you have reached your conclusions.

Your final role in the answer is to explain what the likely outcome of the case would be if it were to proceed to court (or in some instances to another dispute resolution mechanism) and the remedies that the client could hope to obtain. The final conclusion to a problem question answer is usually your assessment of what the client should do in respect of the case – take it to court, settle it out of court or drop the case altogether.

A typical, if complicated, public law problem question would look something like this:

Parliament has introduced a new licensing scheme to make sure that all individuals who want to work as art dealers must hold a licence. Parliament passes the Art Dealers Licensing Act 2015 and the Act states that the new Licensing Authority is responsible for administering the Art Dealers' licensing scheme. Section 2 states that 'The Licensing Authority may issue a licence to an individual to act as an art dealer if the individual has not been convicted of a serious criminal offence and if the individual has a recognised qualification in an art-related subject'. The Act further states that a degree in art or art history from a UK university will automatically be recognised for the purposes of the Act. Interim arrangements exist which require current art dealers to apply for a licence within six months of entry into force of the Act.

The following events occur:
Ruth works for an art dealer in London. Ruth is not sure whether she needs a licence as she currently does not sell art, she only values it. She has no criminal convictions and has a degree in art history from a UK university. She applies to the Licensing Authority for a licence, just in case she needs to have one. Her application is refused. The Authority writes to tell her that she must stop her work immediately as she does not have the required qualification and she is not a fit and proper person to be an art dealer. In the letter the Authority tells her that the decision is final and cannot be challenged in any court whatsoever. Ruth telephones the Licensing Authority to see whether she really needs a licence and speaks to John, the decision-maker. In the course of the conversation he lets slip that he considers that women do not make good art dealers or valuers. Ruth seeks legal advice from you.

The professional publication for art dealers runs an article in their journal about Ruth's situation. A reader of the publication, Phillip, hears of the problem and approaches Ruth to let her know that he would be willing to challenge the decision on her behalf as he is a dealer who has female employees working for him and he is scandalised by what he has heard of her case.

Advise Ruth about her case and Phillip's suggestion to her about his role in bringing an action on her behalf.

The problem is typical in that it asks the student to advise some of the people, the parties or clients, in the scenario; in this instance Ruth and via Ruth also Phillip. It also gives the student most of the factual information needed to provide an assessment of the likely chances of success or failure in a legal action.

The student's role is usually that of a barrister, who is providing a legal opinion, pre-issue of proceedings to the party's solicitor, which the solicitor may share with the client. The opinion should provide the solicitor and client with the information that is needed in order to make a decision on whether they should pursue the action (through negotiation, mediation, arbitration or the courts, as appropriate) or whether they should drop the case as it is unlikely to succeed. The student is not acting as an advocate for the purposes of this exercise. This is very important. If the student were acting as an advocate, as in a moot exchange, for example, then s/he would be trying to make the best case possible for Ruth to the judge. The student would be downplaying any inconvenient legal points and evidence that the other side may rely on. In this instance, the student provides an unvarnished account to allow the client to decide what steps to take next. It is important to present the information for and against Ruth's case, to permit her to make an informed choice.

Chapter 3 will provide a structure you may follow to assist you in answering problem questions. It will take you through the process, step by step, and suggest ways in which you may phrase your answer.

1 A dissertation is an extended piece of writing that is the culmination of in-depth research.

2 It is usual for the student to set the question, rather than to research and write a dissertation to a preset question.

3 **The dissertation takes the reader through relevant points, themes and/or sub-questions, providing research evidence to back up competing viewpoints and providing a final answer to the question.**

4 **It is similar to an essay in nature, but usually requires more detailed research and a longer discussion of the issues.**

THE PURPOSE OF AN EXTENDED RESEARCH ESSAY OR DISSERTATION

A dissertation is an extended piece of writing – often 8,000 to 10,000 words long at undergraduate level, or 15,000 words or more at postgraduate level – which allows a student to explore an area of interest to them and to write an answer to a question that the student has posed. It is not a collection of information on a topic nor a detailed report on the law, but it is a form of extended essay. Many books have been written on how to research and write dissertations and you may wish to refer to some of these if you are engaged in dissertation research. Chapter 4 considers how to approach, structure and write an extended research essay or dissertation, but does not consider the research process in any detail. A dissertation will require far more in-depth research than would a standard essay, but a student would normally still follow the writing and referencing conventions for other forms of legal writing. In addition, dissertation students tend to be more focused in their writing if they have set themselves a question prior to carrying out the main phase of their research. This is discussed further in Chapter 4.

Hopefully you understand the purpose of essays, problem question answers and dissertations. The next stage is to understand how you will be marked for them. The next chapter will explain the criteria that may be used to assess and grade your work. After that, we move on to specific types of written work, before turning our attention to how to undertake the research required to provide evidence to back up the points that you make. You will also need to reference this evidence correctly, to give appropriate credit to the sources of the evidence, but also to demonstrate that you have thoroughly researched the area. Once your written work is completed in draft, it will need to be finished and polished. There is a chapter on preparation for exams, which often come towards the end of the academic year, after coursework has been completed. Finally, we consider what you should take from the mark and feedback that you have received. It is important to learn what you can from your past performance to develop your potential for future written work, legal scholarship and legal practice. An important part of being a professional is reflective practice.

1

HOW TO DO WELL IN ASSESSMENTS

Students tend to focus on assessments rather than on the extent to which they are developing their knowledge of law and their ability to communicate and use that knowledge in writing (and orally). This tends to frustrate academics, who do not feel that assessments are the 'be all and end all' of the learning experience at university. However, students' preoccupation with assessments is understandable, as it is the assessments that determine the degree classification you will achieve. Related to this, once out of university an employer may ask first what grades you have got before discussing the skills and qualities you have as a person. By looking at the way you will be assessed by your lecturer, you should be able to improve your performance and concentrate a little more on what you are learning rather than on how you are being tested. It is less of a mystery than you think. And many of us design assessments so that they may be a tool to help you to learn the important skills and qualities (and, yes, the law too) and not just as an assessment of your learning. This chapter will take you through an example of assessment and grading criteria that may be similar to the ones that will be used to assess your work, to help you to understand what lecturers are looking for. It is worth checking the assessment and grading criteria for your institution too, because each institution will have subtly different ways of wording its criteria even if we are largely attempting to assess similar things.

It is important to bear in mind that assessments are a way of indicating your current level of knowledge and skill. They are not an end in themselves, but a way for you to see how far along the learning journey you have come, and the direction you need to take for the next phase. Completing the assessment is a major hurdle, but it is only the first of many. After that, you need to take the time to assess how well you have demonstrated your knowledge and skill levels and make adjustments to what you will now realise to be your draft assessment. This will improve your chances of success when you submit your final version. Once you receive your feedback, you embark upon the next stage of development, that is, to take the positive and negative comments (and the mark) as guidance for what you need to do to improve your skills and your legal knowledge. These stages form part of a continuous learning cycle through which you will improve your diagnosis, research, legal writing, analysis, argumentation and communication skills. We shall begin right at the beginning, with the need to start with a clear idea.

1.1: STARTING OUT WITH A CLEAR IDEA

To maximise your chances of achieving a good mark in an assessed piece of work, you should have:

1 **an understanding of the specific task that has been set (from the question and/or instructions for the assessment);**

2 **an understanding of how the written work will be assessed (assessment criteria);**

3 **an understanding of how the written work will be graded (grading criteria).**

This chapter will take you through these stages – the way in which you are likely to be assessed and how to maximise your chances of achieving good marks at this stage of writing your answer. It may be helpful to think of it in these terms. If you were an advocate and you were about to go into court to represent a client in a serious criminal case, you would want to know a little about the way in which the court process will work and the way that the judge and the jury will decide upon your client's fate, in order to know how best to prepare your case. You would not go into court without an understanding of how the case will be decided and how your presentation is likely to be judged. Similarly, you should not embark upon an assessment without understanding how you were to be assessed.

How you will be assessed is a clue to how to answer the essay or problem question.

Most courses have published assessment criteria. If they are not in your course or module handbook, then ask for a copy of them from your lecturer. The criteria are really the key to understanding how you need to approach the task set. They are also the key to knowing what skill and knowledge requirements are expected of you at your level of study. All law schools are required to meet the Quality Assurance Agency (QAA) Law Benchmark standards. These set out the threshold skills and qualities of mind that must be attained so as to reach a bare pass at LLB (Hons) level (or equivalent combined degree). The law-specific requirements are as follows:

QAA Law Benchmarks 2015 (page 7)

available at: www.qaa.ac.uk/publications/information-and-guidance/
publication?PubID=2966#.Vcn6YOFRHIU

2.4 A graduate of law with honours has demonstrated:

i intellectual independence including ability to ask and answer cogent questions about law and legal systems, identify gaps in their own knowledge and acquire new knowledge, and engage in critical analysis and evaluation

ii self-management, including an ability to reflect on their own learning, make effective use of feedback, a willingness to acknowledge and correct errors and an ability to work collaboratively

iii awareness of principles and values of law and justice, and of ethics

iv knowledge and understanding of theories, concepts, values, principles and rules of public and private laws within an institutional, social, national and global context

v study in depth and context of substantive areas of law

vi ability to conduct self-directed research including accurate identification of issue(s) which require researching, retrieval and evaluation of accurate, current and relevant information from a range of appropriate sources including primary legal sources

vii ability to work with a range of data, including textual, numerical and statistical

viii ability to recognise ambiguity and deal with uncertainty in law

ix ability to produce a synthesis of relevant doctrinal and policy issues, presentation of a reasoned choice between alternative solutions and critical judgement of the merits of particular arguments

x ability to apply knowledge and understanding to offer evidenced conclusions, addressing complex actual or hypothetical problems

xi ability to communicate both orally and in writing, in relation to legal matters, including an ability to listen and respond to written and oral stimuli including questions and instructions

xii engagement with their own personal and professional development, and academic integrity.

Many of the skills and qualities of mind above will be tested through essay questions, problem questions (actual or hypothetical ones), reports, case notes and other written tasks, although some will be tested through oral presentations too.

The Law Benchmarks make it clear that you have to be able to: diagnose (work out the issues to be treated from the question); to find relevant material (research); to read and understand primary and other sources (including legislation and cases); to use material in context and with reference to material you have learned previously (so you cannot ignore things you have learned in other modules); analyse and synthesise material, meaning that you must be able to pull together multiple forms of authority such as legislation and cases, consider them, draw out their similarities and differences and then use your new understanding of the law so as to reach your own conclusion, whether that is your own analysis as regards a client's case, or in relation to a statement posed in an essay question. And you have to be able to demonstrate that you can do these things on your own without help from lecturers and others. Consequently, you will need to develop your traditional legal skills, your research skills, your analysis skills, your writing skills, your referencing skills and your communication and presentation skills too. Strong written work will combine elements of all of these: it is not enough to know the law and be able to explain someone else's understanding of the law. One must be able to find it, understand it, use it to reach your own conclusions and persuade others that you are correct with reference to multiple sources of authority. And so this book will take a broad interpretation of 'writing' in keeping with the spirit of the Law Benchmark standards.

How do the Law Benchmarks appear in practice in your degree programme? Law schools convert the benchmark standards into assessment and grading criteria that allow academics to assess student performance. Different assessments will have different purposes; they will not all test all of the requirements in the Law Benchmarks. Assessment criteria will normally select a range of issues to address; an example of assessment criteria at level 4 (first-year undergraduate level) is as follows:[1]

---

1 These are generic assessment criteria adapted from those used by the University of Westminster LLB for public law level 4 assessments (first year undergraduate).

Assessment criteria for coursework assessed by essay

In this assessment the student should write an essay plan and an essay in answer to the question.

In the essay students should:

- address the question asked;

- identify the relevant areas with precision;

- demonstrate a thorough knowledge and understanding of the relevant principles, including an analysis of them;

- show evidence of research and reading;

- present a coherent argument for the position taken;

- present work that is well written and structured;

- correctly reference others' work where used.

In the essay plan students should:

- show evidence of having dissected the question;

- show evidence of having identified relevant issues;

- provide headings to indicate the content of each paragraph;

- indicate relevant material under paragraph headings;

- provide a structure for the essay.

The assessment criteria make it clear that for this assessment there are two parts to the written phase of this assessment – an essay plan and an essay – and that both parts have their own assessment criteria. The criteria demonstrate that the marker is looking for different things from the two parts. It is important that the criteria are met for each. They are testing your ability to use different skills. To achieve a strong mark in this assessment a student would have to write an essay plan that is split into sections indicating the content of each paragraph. The plan should show that the student has read the question and dissected it so that s/he can understand and answer it. The essay is a continuation of the plan; in other words it follows the plan but is written in full sentences and paragraphs rather than in note form. The essay should address the question posed, and it should demonstrate that the student has understood the principles relevant to the question and has constructed arguments and cited evidence to back up arguments relevant to answering the question. This evidence is a product of research carried out by the student prior to writing the essay.

The assessment criteria for the exam assessment are slightly different again. In this example students must answer three questions from a paper containing six questions made up of a mix of essay questions and problem questions. Students are assessed against the following:

Assessment criteria for exam written answers[1]

A student should:

- identify relevant issues and principles in respect of the question;

- demonstrate knowledge of the relevant principles and give examples where appropriate;

- apply the principles in their answer;

- demonstrate an understanding of and answer the question;

- apply statutory and judicial material in any hypothetical factual situations;

- demonstrate an ability to answer questions in exam conditions with appropriate regard to timing;

- communicate in good English.

1 Once again, these criteria are adapted from those used in LLB public law level 4 exams at the University of Westminster, as are the grading criteria that appear later in this chapter.

The criteria are similar to those for the coursework, but they are set slightly differently. Essays and problem questions written in closed-book exams (exams in which you are not permitted to refer to any materials in the exam room) are a test of knowledge and the ability to apply that knowledge to answer the question, rather than such a test of a student's research ability. Students need to be clear about the general principles of law in a given area and the evidence that supports those general principles prior to entering the exam. Once in the exam, a student would need to dissect the question, plan an answer and apply the general principles. Exam technique is discussed in more detail in Chapter 8; however, the important point here is to be sure about how you will be assessed prior to embarking upon the assessed task.

Your essay or problem question answer, or plan, will be read in the light of the criteria and how you do will depend on how far you have met the criteria. Many courses also have grading criteria, which the marker will use in conjunction with the assessment criteria to work out your mark. Grading criteria do vary, so be sure to check the grading criteria that are used in your law school. Two examples are provided by the Higher Education Funding Council for England (HEFCE) QAA Benchmark Statements for Law 2007. This document has been a point of reference for law schools since 2007, and so although criteria may vary from institution to institution, it is likely that most law schools will have drawn upon these examples and be looking for similar levels of attainment at each of the grade boundaries. In this chapter we focus on the example of grading criteria set out in Appendix C, which have been considered to be an example of good practice in a legal context by the QAA. Each band of grading criteria sets out the minimum levels of attainment that a student will have achieved at the point when they graduate from a law honours degree (usually a LLB degree, but it could be a Graduate Diploma/CPE programme, too). Many institutions will expect a lesser standard at level 4 (first year) and level 5 (second year) than they do at level 6 (third and usually graduating year). Consequently the QAA criteria may be set a little higher than those that are being used in your institution in your first and second year of studies. However, it is important to aim high at level 4 so that you have a good grasp of the basic skills and develop the qualities that you need in order to excel in your level 5 and 6 years. This allows you to spend more time on honing your skills and also on conducting detailed research and critical analysis that should result in you achieving high marks. It is better to learn the skills as soon as possible, so that you may concentrate on perfecting them while conducting detailed research and excellent written work for your other assessments.

A third-class answer at level 6, one that falls into the 40–49% boundary, will have been assessed as set out in the box below.

3rd (40–49%)

This assessment will demonstrate a basic understanding of the main issues but not coherently or correctly presented.

Third-class answers demonstrate some knowledge or understanding of the general area but a third class answer tends to be weak in the following ways:

- **descriptive only;**

- **does not answer the question directly;**

- **misses key points;**

- **contains important inaccuracies;**

- **covers material sparsely, possibly in note form;**

- **assertions not supported by authority or evidence.**

A student will achieve a mark of 40–49% if s/he identifies the subject area that the question addresses and writes something that is relevant to the question. The assessment will also meet the minimum standards of presentation. It will demonstrate that the student is familiar with the subject area. A student who achieves a third-class mark has missed key points raised by the question, and his or her answer may also contain some important inaccuracies. There is a real lack of evidence in support of the points being made. The assessment is also largely descriptive, meaning that the student has simply repeated what someone else has said or written, rather than thinking about what this means and providing his or her own thoughts (analysis). This would be similar to being an advocate for the defence in a murder case, to stand before the jury and to explain a little bit about the history of the law of murder and what the law states as regards the offence of murder, before sitting back down again. The jury would be none the wiser about whether or not the defendant had anything to do with the murder and the barrister would not have presented evidence to them to help them to make up their own minds. A written answer along these lines would be fairly basic and would benefit from a clearer understanding of what the question was asking. A student with a mark at this level should concentrate on the first essay writing stage set out in the next chapter – considering the nature of the question, before starting the research and writing phases.

A student will achieve a 2.2 mark for his or her assessment if the written work is judged to meet the following criteria.

2.2 (50–59%)

This assessment provides a substantially correct answer, which shows an understanding of the basic principles.

Lower second-class answers display an acceptable level of competence, as indicated by the following qualities:

- **generally accurate;**

- **providing an adequate answer to the question based largely on text-books and lecture notes;**

- clearly presented;

- no real development of arguments;

- may contain some major error or omission;

- a lower second-class answer may also be a good answer (i.e. an upper second-class answer) to a related question but not one set by the examiner.

A student will achieve a mark of 50–59% if s/he correctly identifies the subject area of the question (as for an essay of 40–49%) but then goes on to discuss the main issue raised in the question as well as some related issues along with some relevant cases, statutes or academic opinion. The cases, statutes or academic opinion (which shows some evidence of reading or research) will have been applied to the question or the facts of the problem question in some way. However, there may not be evidence of extensive research. A student will have constructed an argument and shown an adequate understanding of the subject area, but without sufficient focus on the question. Students who achieve a mark of 50–59% should concentrate on identifying the issues relevant to the question and using their research findings to construct an argument to answer the question. This is discussed more in the next chapter.

2.1 (60–69%)

An upper second-class answer generally shows a sound understanding of both the basic principles and the relevant details of the law, supported by examples that are demonstrably well understood and which are presented in a coherent and logical fashion.

The answer should be well presented, display some analytical ability and contain no major errors or omissions. It will not necessarily be excellent in any area.

Upper second class answers cover a wider band of students. Such answers are clearly highly competent and typically possess the following qualities:

- generally accurate and well-informed;

- reasonably comprehensive;

- well organised and structured;

- provide evidence of general reading;

- demonstrating a sound grasp of basic principles;

- demonstrating a good understanding of the relevant details;

- succinctly and cogently presented;

- displaying some evidence of insight.

One essential aspect of an upper second-class answer is that it must have competently dealt with the question asked by the examiner.

A student who achieves a mark of 60–69% has correctly identified the subject of the question and has also identified most of the relevant issues. In addition, s/he has also cited most of the relevant material that is the subject of the question, having constructed arguments and provided a judgement on differing viewpoints. A student who has achieved a mark in this classification will have demonstrated a good understanding of the subject area, and will have applied that knowledge to the question posed. S/he will also have provided an appropriate conclusion to the question or scenario. A student who wishes to improve should concentrate on developing his or her analysis of each issue by adding a sentence at the end of each paragraph stating why and how the issue is relevant to the question as well as deepening his or her understanding of the subject area by undertaking further reading. In many instances a 2.1 answer may be improved to become a first-class answer through additional research and redrafting so as to allow the student to develop more sophisticated arguments and conclusions. This is discussed in more detail in the forthcoming chapters.

1st (70%+)

A first-class answer has a thoughtful structure, a clear message displaying personal reflection informed by wider reading of articles and/or other commentaries and a good grasp of detail (as evidenced by the choice of relevant examples which are well integrated into the answer's structure). Complete with no errors or omissions.

First-class answers are ones that are exceptionally good for an undergraduate and which excel in at least one and probably several of the following criteria:

- comprehensiveness and accuracy;

- clarity of argument and expression;

- integration of a range of materials;

- evidence of wider reading;

- insight into the theoretical issues.

Excellence in one or more of these areas should be in addition to the qualities expected of an upper second-class answer. Although there is no expectation of originality of exposition or treatment, a first-class answer is generally expected to spot points rarely seen. A high first (75+%) is expected to display originality and excel in most if not all the aforementioned criteria.

As shown above, a first-class answer has to demonstrate a very high level of knowledge and skill, but it is possible to achieve if a student really understands a topic, has conducted in-depth research on the topic and has properly dissected the question and written to it. The criteria indicate that a student is not expected to come up with a new legal theory or to find a completely different way of looking at the law. However, the essay does need to be focused to answer the question, with evidence to back up all the points being made within it. It also needs to be comprehensive and extremely well written.

Not all criteria will necessary apply equally in every type of coursework or examination or with equal weight; for example, in a written examination the evidence of independent research required may be less than in coursework. Your course will have slightly different criteria and you should check what these are if you are unsure of how you will be graded, or if you do not understand why you have received the mark you have been given for an assessed essay or problem question answer. You should attempt to aim as high as possible, rather than aiming at a bare pass. It sounds obvious, but it is surprising how many students aim at the pass rather than at the higher end of the marking spectrum! Apart from anything else, on a law programme you will use the same skills over and over again. The sooner that you learn how to make good use of the key legal writing and research skills, the more you will get out of your law degree experience. This is likely to mean that you will also enjoy your time on the course rather more, too. Plus, the sooner you learn the skills that you need, the more time you can spend on focusing on the detail of each assessment rather than the basics. And the more time you will have to take your focus off assessment and to explore the law and to enjoy doing so.

As you will have seen from the criteria, the next important stage in the writing process is to dissect the question or problem question scenario to make sure that you have identified the task that has been set for you. If you are writing a dissertation and must formulate a question of your own, follow this stage once you have developed your question with the help of your supervisor. More information is given on formulating questions for dissertations in Chapter 4. The research phase, including reading your lecture and tutorial notes, should focus on the question rather than on the topic in general terms. By focusing on the question you give yourself the best chance of achieving the highest mark possible. This is discussed further in the next chapter.

Next steps:

You may wish to look back through any previous assessed written work that you have done on your law course. Look at the mark and the comments that you received and consider what we have covered in this chapter. Do you understand why you got the mark that you got? Can you see what you would need to do to improve?

You may also wish to read through the example short essay provided below and grade it in the light of what you have learnt in this chapter. You may compare your thoughts against the mark and comments given to the work, towards the back of the book.

You may wish to examine the assessment criteria and the grading criteria that will be used to assess you for your next piece of coursework (or exam). This should help you to prepare for the assessment, to develop your legal and transferable skills, and to maximise your chances of success.

You may want to consider how you structure and present your work as these factors will have an impact on the grade you are awarded.

You may also wish to refer to Chapter 5 (research and making use of evidence), Chapter 6 (referencing and citations), Chapter 7 (finishing and polishing your work) and Chapter 9 (feedback and how to use it).

1.2: APPLY YOUR KNOWLEDGE OF ASSESSMENT CRITERIA

Read through the brief essay below and consider what mark you would give to it, based on the limitation that the essay should be about 500 words in length. Refer back to the assessment criteria and then set out your reasons for giving the mark you have awarded. Check the mark you have awarded and your reasons for the mark against the ones given in the answers section towards the back of the book. You may wish to try to rephrase the paragraphs so as to enhance the answer, and then check the guidance on the companion website on essay writing prior to remaking your own effort. You may also wish to do the exercises on the companion website, where you will find more examples including those covering some other areas of law.

'The British Parliament was once supreme.' Discuss with reference to Britain's membership of the EU and its obligations in relation to the European Convention on Human Rights.

This issue of parliamentary sovereignty has been that Parliament has been sovereign throughout centuries until the UK joined the European Community (European Communities Act 1972). Theorists such as Dicey have argued that Parliament is so powerful and so totally sovereign that it is allowed to do anything that it wishes, even to order that smoking on the streets of Paris could be outlawed by the UK Parliament. However, there are those who disagree with this and the essay will consider opinions for and against whether Parliament is supreme or not.

It may be considered that sovereignty has been lost from Parliament. This is because Britain joined Europe and Europe's power overtook the power of the British Parliament. This was done through the enactment of the ECA 1972. Many are of the belief that the Act is now entrenched, that Parliament cannot repeal it. There was a recent case about this where a man wanted to weigh his fruit and vegetables in pounds and was told he could not because Europe says that we must all use kilogrammes and grammes. This shows that Parliament is no longer supreme.

However, there is a dispute about this point. The case of British Railways Board v. Pickin demonstrates that no Act of Parliament can be held to be invalid. This suggests that the courts must apply a British Act of Parliament and that Parliament can enact any law that it wishes; as long as the Act is passed it will become law in this country.

However, the Factortame case in the 1990s shows another side to this situation as the British courts did not apply the British Act of Parliament – the Merchant Shipping Act – but they applied the European law instead as they had been told they must by the European Court of Justice.

Theorists such as Dicey consider Parliament to be supreme. The European Convention on Human Rights now means that Parliament cannot pass any law that is against the Human Rights Act and so this means that Parliament is no longer supreme. However, Parliament was the body that enacted the Human Rights Act and it can repeal the Act and so Parliament is still supreme in the sense that it has only temporarily limited its power.

In conclusion, parliamentary sovereignty may exist as Parliament can repeal the ECA 1972 and the HRA 1998, but the power of Parliament to legislate has been limited by joining Europe and the ECHR and therefore Dicey's theory of sovereignty is not totally correct.

[417 words]

SUMMARY

To maximise your chances of achieving a good mark in an assessed piece of work, you should:

Have an understanding of the specific task that has been set (from the question and/or instructions for the assessment)

↓

Have read through the instructions given with the assessment and be clear on them

↓

Have made sure you have all the information you need about the assessment format, regulations and deadline

↓

Have an understanding of how the written work will be assessed, having read through the assessment criteria

↓

Have an understanding of how the written work will be graded, having read through the grading criteria

↓

Once you are clear on the task that has been set you may move on to the next phase, as set out in Chapters 2, 3 and 4

2   ESSAY WRITING

It is hard to know where to start when it comes to writing an essay or an answer to a problem question. Students often say that the most difficult stage of writing is to begin, and many academics find this as well with their own writing. When one has lots of ideas, it is difficult to sift through what should be left out and what should be included, and to work out how to put those ideas down on paper. The easiest way may be to split the process up into stages and to work through each one in turn without worrying about the next until you have completed the last one. This chapter will consider how to approach writing an essay. It could properly be argued that we should consider first the nature of legal research and use of research sources before we move on to consider essay writing. However, as I hope I shall demonstrate below, it is important that research is used as part of the writing process rather than a precursor to it. You need to be clear on the task that you have been set, and also on what you know already, before you begin undertaking research and before you plan your answer. Please do follow up your reading of this chapter by also turning to the chapters on research, referencing and finishing and polishing your work too. It may also be as well to reread the first chapter on how you will be assessed, once you have a first draft of your essay.

2.1: STAGE 1: READ THE QUESTION

> - **You are marked on how well you have answered the question.**
>
> - **Make sure you know what task you have been set.**
>
> - **You need to spend some time working out what the question is asking you to do.**

You should never begin to write until you understand the task that you have been set. Writing in a state of confusion will lead to a confused piece of writing and a lower mark than you would hope to achieve. One way to make sure that you are clear on what the question is asking you to do is to rewrite the question in different words, or to write out the main subject of the question followed by the specific points you must address in order to answer the question fully. You may need to expand on the title in order to make sense of it. A typical essay title would be something like this:

'The British Parliament was once supreme.' Discuss with reference to Britain's membership of the EU and its obligations in relation to the European Convention on Human Rights (ECHR).

The essay is asking you to address a number of issues. The main subject of the question is parliamentary supremacy (sometimes known as 'sovereignty' as indicated in the quotation). This should be the principal subject of your essay. The essay question asks you to discuss parliamentary supremacy, but it also instructs you to consider two issues in particular in your discussion: Britain's membership of the EU and its obligations in relation to the ECHR. Your answer must consider these issues in the light of parliamentary supremacy. It is important that you focus on these issues. Look up any words in the question of which you are unsure, in order that you are clear before you dissect the question as below. Each word will be in the question for a reason.

So, the question looks something like this, when split up into its constituent parts:

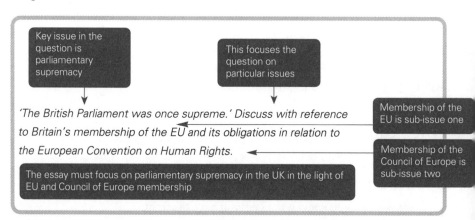

Do look at the additional examples provided on the companion website, where you will also be able to test your ability to dissect questions too. And if you are in any way unsure about what words such as 'analyse', 'discuss', 'critically assess', etc. mean at the end of essay questions then do revisit the introduction for further guidance, where these terms are discussed.

It may help to rewrite the question in your own words (or display it as a mind map or flow chart), for clarity, but do ensure that your version really is similar to the one that has been set. Answering an alternative question will likely reduce your essay mark to one in the 2.2 range or lower, regardless of how good an answer it is to your question. It is important to bear in mind that not every question has a cut-and-dried answer. Some questions are truly arguable, and open to a variety of different interpretations and answers. These tend to provide some students with the opportunity to show off their abilities, but they may trip up some students too. They should be approached in similar ways to standard questions but need to be dissected with great care so that you do not wander off the point. Before moving on, check that you have read any instructions that have been provided with the essay: word length, deadline, any compulsory reading, etc. It is also worth checking the assessment criteria (as discussed in Chapter 1). You are ready to move on to the next stage of writing once you are clear about the task you have been set.

2.2: STAGE 2: READ THROUGH YOUR NOTES AND MAKE A LIST OF RELEVANT ISSUES

Read through any lecture or tutorial notes that you already have on the topic. Make a list of issues from your notes that appear to relate to the question.

Research the main issues for the subject area and take notes from your textbook, if you have not read around the area already.

Carry out further research: you need to look at more than the textbook and the case book to write a good essay.

- **You should consider other books, journal articles and official publications as well as primary legal sources such as cases and legislation.**

- **The reading list in the module handbook will give you some ideas of what reading you need to do and where to look for evidence.**

See Chapter 5 for tips on how to make the most of your reading and how to use research material in your written work. Remember that any notes you take should be focused on the question rather than general notes on the topic.

Refer back to the question frequently during your reading, to make sure that you remain focused on it.

Begin with your existing information sources including any lecture, seminar or tutorial notes that are on the point, as well as any textbook reading or further reading that you have done on the principal subject of the essay. Use this material in the first instance and consider whether any of it could be useful in your essay. Then conduct your own research (see Chapter 5 for assistance with this) and make targeted notes that contain material directly relevant to the question. You need to work out which issues are relevant to your question. It is a tricky stage to explain, as the issues are specific to the title that has been set. Having said that, there are hints about relevant issues and these should be set out in your lectures on the topic that forms the subject of the assessment. Similarly, it is likely that the key issues on a given topic have been discussed in your tutorial or seminar on the area. Finally, the key issues will be set out in your textbook reading, which may have been set as pre-reading for your tutorial. Key issues are principles or concepts; they are not details or reams of facts. Key issues would include the general principles of offer and acceptance in contract law, or principles that must be demonstrated in order to prove negligence in tort law. They are the building blocks of the topic. In relation to the question above, they will be the theories of parliamentary supremacy in public law and how the established theories of supremacy have been affected by membership of the EU or signature of the ECHR. Cases, statutes and the detail of individual theories are all evidence of the key principles or concepts rather than the principles or concepts themselves and it is important that you make that distinction. At this stage you are describing what you have read that you believe to be relevant to answering the question.

You should take notes on the key principles and concepts that form the basis of the question topic, but only include enough information so that you are able to understand the principle along with any evidence that supports differing views of that principle. Try to avoid including lots of other information, as this will simply confuse the issue when you come to plan and to write your essay. In note terms, less may very well mean more marks. Please also make sure that you are clear on whether you are summarising others' words (paraphrasing) or quoting their words directly. You will need to keep a note of the full citation (see Chapter 6 for details) including the page number from which you have found the ideas or the words that you are noting down. This is important, because when you come to reread your notes and begin to write you must be able to distinguish between your ideas, your words and others' ideas and others' words.

> **When taking notes be sure to:**
>
> • either quote directly from the text that you are reading. Use quotation marks, note down the full citation for the quote including page numbers; or
>
> • properly summarise in your own words the ideas that you have read in the text, taking a note of the full citation including the page number; and
>
> • keep a full and accurate reference for each source you use including the page number for the page on which you found the material. You will need this information for your footnotes later.

It is much easier to write a proper summary if you read and reread the paragraph or phrase and then put the text to one side and think about how you would explain the idea in your own words. You should not use the author's original phrase or make a few word changes as this is not a proper paraphrase, but is instead merely a poor quote. You must make a distinction between explaining others' ideas in your own words, and using others' words in quotation format. Many students who are given feedback that they are guilty of 'poor scholarship' will have half summarised and half copied others' words into their notes and then again copied those notes into their essay. They may not realise that they have stolen someone else's words and/or ideas with attribution, and the root cause for the problem was poor note-taking rather than an intention to plagiarise.

2.3: STAGE 3: ORGANISE YOUR IDEAS INTO A LOGICAL ORDER

> • This is a form of essay plan.
>
> • List the issues and number each one or note each issue in a separate mind-map bubble.
>
> • Write a sentence next to each issue to explain what the issue is.
>
> • Note down any evidence you will use to support your discussion of the issue (cases, quotes, etc.) under each issue.
>
> • Check that the issues are in a logical order.

This stage helps you to begin to understand the material that you have read, to order it into key themes or points and to structure it as well as to capture your early thoughts. You are moving from describing – reporting what you have read and know to be relevant to the question – to analysing – ordering what you have understood from what you have read and giving an indication of how you believe it to be relevant to your answer.

There are many different ways of organising your ideas. Some people draw mind maps or other forms of diagrams. Others jot down ideas in no particular order, and then rearrange them over time. However, some people prefer a structured text-based approach that they can follow until they come up with a personalised way of organising their material. This is one suggestion as to how to do this. You could make a list of issues that you will discuss in your essay from your notes, but these will be in no particular order. The easiest way to sort them out is to leave them in a list for now (with large gaps in between each issue) and to write a sentence after each issue that explains what the issue is about, like so:

'The British Parliament was once supreme.' Discuss with reference to Britain's membership of the EU and its obligations in relation to the European Convention on Human Rights.

1 **Introduction**

2 **Basic definition of parliamentary supremacy** – This is the term given to a collection of theories that explain that the British Parliament has the supreme power to legislate, to amend and to repeal law in the country.

3 **Theories of parliamentary supremacy** – The differing theories of supremacy suggest that Parliament has different roles and different levels of power to legislate depending on the theorist's view of Parliament.

4 **Parliamentary supremacy and the EU:** Parliament is no longer supreme – There is evidence to suggest that as a result of Britain's membership of the EU, Parliament is no longer supreme.

5 **Parliamentary supremacy and the EU:** Parliament remains supreme – There is evidence to suggest that as a result of Britain's membership of the EU, Parliament remains supreme.

6 **Parliamentary supremacy and the ECHR:** Parliament is no longer supreme – There is evidence to suggest that Parliament lost its supremacy once Britain signed the ECHR.

> 7 **Parliamentary supremacy and the ECHR:** Parliament remains supreme –
> There is evidence to suggest that Parliament is still supreme even after
> Britain signed the ECHR.
>
> 8 **Conclusion**

The next stage is to list any evidence you have that relates to the issues – a case, a statutory reference, a quotation or an idea from an academic work. If these point in different directions then, for now, group the ones that support a view of that issue and those that are against a view of that issue. For example, for point 4 on the list:

> 4 **Parliamentary supremacy and the EU: Parliament is no longer supreme**
> – There is evidence to suggest that as a result of Britain's membership of
> the EU, Parliament is no longer supreme.
>
> European Communities Act 1972 [see notes].
>
> Discussion of *Factortame* case on the hierarchy of UK and EU law [see
> notes].
>
> Reference to Hilaire Barnett's book *Constitutional and Administrative Law*
> on this point [see notes].

Then write a sentence at the bottom of that issue heading, stating how you think this issue may be relevant to the question, or what it means as regards the question. For example:

> 4 **Parliamentary supremacy and the EU: Parliament is no longer**
> **supreme – There is evidence to suggest that as a result of Britain's**
> **membership of the EU, Parliament is no longer supreme.**
>
> European Communities Act 1972 [see notes].
>
> Discussion of *Factortame* case on the hierarchy of UK and EU law [see
> notes].
>
> Reference to Hilaire Barnett's book *Constitutional and Administrative Law*
> [see notes] on this point.
>
> This indicates that where there is a direct conflict between British law and
> European law then European law will prevail, thus suggesting that the British
> Parliament is no longer supreme, as European law is hierarchically superior.

Remember to remind yourself of the question at regular intervals to ensure that you are not wandering off the point. Also, consider whether you need to conduct more research so as to deepen your evidence base (see Chapter 5 for more details, if you are unsure) and to provide a more sophisticated analysis. Analysis is simply your assessment of any given issue (your opinion, to an extent), but it must be based on sound evidence. Consequently, if you are making a point and yet you have little (authoritative) evidence in support of the point that you are making, then you will need to conduct more research. Evidence is sometimes referred to as 'authority' in a legal context, meaning cases and legislation. This material will need to be properly referenced in foot-notes, as will all other evidence. You will need to read these sources in their original form rather than relying on summaries in textbooks and from the lectures. Your research and your assessment of what that authority means in the light of the question, is the key to strong analysis.

Continue with the planning process until you have exhausted all the issues on your list. You should now have a whole series of issues with a sentence explaining each issue, evidence that you could use in a discussion of the issue and a sentence explaining each issue's relevance to the question. Read through your plan and consider whether any of the issues need to be reordered to assist the flow of your ideas. Do some follow on from others? Are some totally unconnected and so need to be kept separate? Consider whether you want to keep evidence for a point or against a point separate (in separate paragraphs). Or will you combine the evidence for and against in a single paragraph so as to provide a more sophisticated and developed argument? You may choose to organise your arguments thematically, according to each point you wish to make, or you may choose to address arguments for a proposition then arguments against a proposition instead. When being asked to critically assess in the question it is as well to combine all evidence on a point in a single paragraph as this will make it easier for you to reach a sophisticated conclusion on that point. But some essay questions may actively encourage you to argue different standpoints in different paragraphs, in compare and contrast, or evaluate questions for example, in which case it may be better to keep the arguments separated. Once you are happy with the order then you are ready to move on to the writing stage of your essay or to your problem question answer.

2.3.1 START WRITING: YOU ARE NOW READY TO BEGIN TO WRITE

You are only now ready to begin to write your answer. It is important that you have first completed the writing stages above, as otherwise you are likely to jump into the middle of the essay and then write around in circles, with no clear idea of what you need to say and how you will attempt to say it. The writing process can be split into small and manageable steps. Good luck with your writing!

2.4: STAGE 4: WRITING YOUR INTRODUCTION

I have put this section here, as many people believe that you should start at the beginning and write your introduction first. However, many of us find this difficult and in fact leave the introduction to the end of our writing process. We shall consider it here, but please bear in mind that you may find it easier to write your introduction (or at least rewrite your introduction) once you have reviewed the first draft of your essay.

> **Set out your approach to answering the question by mentioning briefly the issues you will cover.**
>
> **If you really cannot do this then you may not be that clear on how you are going to approach answering the question. Go back to the question to check that you understand the task that you have been set.**

Your introduction may now be relatively easy to write as your introduction is simply a paragraph in which you set out the task that you have been set (very briefly) and you explain the issues that you will deal with in your answer. You should be able to do this from the plan that you developed at stage 3 above. An introduction is merely a signpost to what is to come. It does not, usually, go into the history or development of the topic in a standard-length essay (as opposed to an introduction in a dissertation). It should be similar to a brief TV trailer or the introductory remarks in a lecture. A simple introduction may look something like this:

> It has been suggested that the British Parliament was once ◄——— supreme, but that its supremacy has been eroded as a result of Britain's membership of the EU and its signature of the European Convention on Human Rights. In order to examine this proposition ◄— it is necessary to consider the definition of parliamentary supremacy and differing theories of supremacy. The essay will consider evidence in respect of Britain's membership of the EU and the extent to which that affects Parliamentary supremacy. The essay will also consider Britain's signature of the European Convention of Human Rights in the same light.

The first sentence sets out the purpose of the essay

The next three sentences set out the issues to be addressed in order to fulfil the task

Some introductions will also conclude by stating the conclusion that the student has reached through her/his research for and writing of the essay. However, as mentioned previously, some people find it much easier to write their introduction towards the end of the writing process, usually once they have a first draft of the main body of the essay. This is because many people make connections between issues and come up with ideas as they are writing. Consider how you understand what it is that you know. Do you make connections and come to answers through talking to people, drawing diagrams or writing text? If it is the last of these, then you may want to postpone your introduction until you have had a first go at writing the essay, as writing the first draft will be a process that helps you to work out what you think. After that, you will need to redraft your essay knowing what you then know, as your essay should read as if you had reached your conclusion before you started to write and thus you were writing from a position of strength rather than so as to work out your answer. But if you prefer to talk through your ideas, or to draw diagrams as an initial step, then you may prefer to begin at the beginning and write your introduction as a first stage, redrafting it frequently as your knowledge develops.

2.5: STAGE 5: WRITING THE MIDDLE SECTION OF YOUR ESSAY

- Organise your ideas into paragraphs. One paragraph should contain one issue.

- At the beginning of each paragraph state what the issue is.

- Develop and discuss the issue within the middle part of the paragraph, by way of justification for the issue set out in the first sentence.

- Provide authoritative evidence for the points you are making and explain how that evidence has helped you to reach your conclusions.

- Finish the paragraph by stating why this issue is relevant to or how it helps you in answering the question.

The middle section of your essay is made up of a series of paragraphs, and each paragraph will correspond to one of the issues that you have set out in your plan at stage 3 above. The middle section of your essay will also be relatively straightforward to write from your plan, if you have followed the stages through in order.

2.5.1 WHAT IS A PARAGRAPH?

A paragraph is a block of text. Some people indent the first line so that it starts slightly further across the page than the rest of the lines in that block of text. Other people prefer to stick to a block of text that begins at the same point on each line, just as this one does. This is increasingly common as people use word processors to write their assessments. If you are unsure about what is accepted practice in your law school, check with your tutor to see if there are guidelines on presentation of work. A paragraph should be a self-contained unit, which means that you should finish off your idea or issue in one block of text before moving on to another. If the paragraph looks to be rather long, then consider whether you have more than one idea or one issue in that one paragraph and split it accordingly.

2.5.2 HOW DO I CONSTRUCT MY PARAGRAPH?

The easiest way to write a paragraph is to stick to a workable formula until you feel comfortable with developing a more personalised style of writing. There are few clear-cut rules about paragraph writing except to say that each para- graph is a communication aimed to persuade the reader that you have reached a strong conclusion on each point. To do this you need to be clear on the point that you are making, why you think you are right (you will need to justify your point by showing how the evidence you have found leads you to your conclusion) and why your point is important as regards the question. One formula that appears to work for students is set out in stage 5. In this approach, the first sentence of your paragraph sets out the issue or point that you will make in the paragraph (your own point that you have worked out to be important, and so it may be better to call it your conclusion on the point). This is likely to be similar to the sentence that you have written in your plan next to the listed issue, at least in your first draft. This sentence explains to the reader what you have worked out, so that the reader knows where they are being taken next. The middle part of a paragraph is the discussion section. The sentences in this part will explain the point by providing the principles and/or concepts associated with it including the evidence you have to support your understanding of these principles. This acts as the justification for how you know you have reached a conclusion (a point) on an issue relevant to the ques- tion. If the issue is relatively uncomplicated, you may be able to put arguments for and against the issue in one paragraph to persuade the reader how you have reached your conclusion (your point). However, if your paragraph looks to be becoming too long, you may wish to split the issue into two paragraphs – one that provides the discussion of the arguments on one side, and another that provides the discussion on the other. Or you may prefer to look again at the point that you are trying to make and consider whether it is really a single point or whether it is a collection of points that may be split over a number of paragraphs. Your paragraph should be rounded off with one or two concluding sentences, which are very important. The concluding sentence explains how and why the point is important in relation to the question. This sentence is an important one as it is your original material and if well considered it may demonstrate your critical analysis (your high-level, well-considered analysis). You have worked out why it is an important point and your analysis, if well founded, should improve your marks as indicated by the assessment criteria in Chapter 1. Analysis is simply your own understanding, or assessment, formed as a result of reviewing authoritative evidence. This is why the research process is such an important one, as your analysis is heavily dependent on the material that you have read and considered, and then converted into analysis by applying your new understanding to the question or sub-question.

An example of a well-written early draft paragraph for point four is as follows, although note that it can be improved further as discussed in the section on use of evidence below:

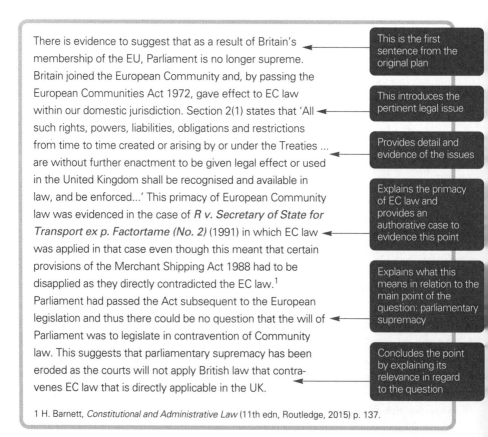

There is evidence to suggest that as a result of Britain's membership of the EU, Parliament is no longer supreme. — This is the first sentence from the original plan

Britain joined the European Community and, by passing the European Communities Act 1972, gave effect to EC law within our domestic jurisdiction. Section 2(1) states that 'All ← This introduces the pertinent legal issue

such rights, powers, liabilities, obligations and restrictions from time to time created or arising by or under the Treaties ... ← Provides detail and evidence of the issues

are without further enactment to be given legal effect or used in the United Kingdom shall be recognised and available in law, and be enforced...' This primacy of European Community law was evidenced in the case of *R v. Secretary of State for Transport ex p. Factortame (No. 2)* (1991) in which EC law ← Explains the primacy of EC law and provides an authoritative case to evidence this point

was applied in that case even though this meant that certain provisions of the Merchant Shipping Act 1988 had to be disapplied as they directly contradicted the EC law.[1]

Parliament had passed the Act subsequent to the European legislation and thus there could be no question that the will of ← Explains what this means in relation to the main point of the question: parliamentary supremacy

Parliament was to legislate in contravention of Community law. This suggests that parliamentary supremacy has been eroded as the courts will not apply British law that contravenes EC law that is directly applicable in the UK. ← Concludes the point by explaining its relevance in regard to the question

1 H. Barnett, *Constitutional and Administrative Law* (11th edn, Routledge, 2015) p. 137.

An example of a less well-written and well-considered paragraph making use of similar material would be as follows:

> **The UK Parliament is no longer supreme. The case of *Factortame* tells us that EC law overrides UK law.[1] This case was about Spanish fishermen wanting to fish in British waters using British fishing quotas. The UK courts ruled that they could not as it was against a piece of UK law that required them to register in the UK in order for them to be able to fish here. But the ECJ ruled that they could as EC law is superior to UK law. This shows that parliamentary supremacy no longer exists where EC law applies.**
>
> 1 Lecture Notes Membership of EU and Parliamentary Supremacy Nov 2014. [Check primary sources via the library.]

This paragraph uses substantially the same basic material as the previous example paragraph and it does introduce the idea to be discussed and provide a conclusion that explains how this paragraph assists in answering the question. So far, it is not too bad. However, the relevant statute is not mentioned nor are the provisions quoted or summarised. Instead, there is only vague reference to the legal provision. The facts of the case are (not terribly effectively) summarised and there is an attempt to explain the important legal principle established by the case of *Factortame (No. 2)*, but the point is not made crisply. The case reference is not complete and, importantly, the '(No. 2)' is missed so we are unclear which of the five *Factortame* cases is being referred to. This is not a terrible paragraph, as its basic anatomy is relatively sound, but it fails to make the best use of the evidence that it seeks to present. And it does not communicate the point as clearly as it could.

Once you have provided your critical analysis you may move on to the next paragraph, which should contain the next issue from your essay plan devised in stage 3. Repeat the pattern until you have exhausted all the issues on your list.

2.6: WHY USE EVIDENCE?

- Evidence adds weight to your arguments. It shows how you know that what you are saying is valid.

- Evidence helps the reader to consider the authority of your points. If you have good evidence in support of what you are saying, that suggests authority. Your arguments may be considered to be less reliable however, if your evidence is sparse or of poor quality (e.g. you have relied on a rather unreliable internet source).

- Try to avoid making an assertion if you do not have the evidence to back it up, as you will lose marks for this.

- Evidence may be found in cases, legislation, authoritative quotes or other reported research findings including green and white papers, policy documents, etc.

- You must reference the sources you have drawn upon in footnotes or endnotes (discussed in Chapter 6).

As indicated above, it is important to have evidence to back up the points that you are making (see Chapter 5, if you are in any doubt about this). But it is also important to bear in mind that your role is not to look for evidence to support your own opinion, your role is to read as widely as possible and to use that material to help you to develop a more scholarly, evidenced opinion. Once you have reached a scholarly opinion your research sources become your evidence base to demonstrate how you reached that opinion. Your opinion is then known as analysis (your conclusions) as it is based on your analysis of the sources you have read. In reality, your research becomes your evidence; it is only by under-taking high quality research that you will develop a good quality understanding of an area, that leads you to be able to make strong arguments supported by high quality evidence (the evidence being material that you have used from the research phase). Indeed, each sentence that asserts an argument or sets out a prin-ciple should contain evidence and a footnote to the source of that evidence.

Evidence is not limited to a set of sources, it may be in the form of cases, statutory references, quotes or ideas from academic work including theories, empirical research findings, and academic opinion on cases or legislation or on how law is working in practice. Newspaper debates or phone polls are evidence of what the public think about an issue, but they are not authoritative accounts of the law. You may use sources such as these to supplement your legal sources if, for example, you are discussing how the law is perceived by the public, but do not use such sources as evidence of what the law is or how judges have decided cases. Your evidence is there to support your analysis and consequently it must prove your point. Further, to be persuasive it needs to be of high quality.

Evidence should be used in the middle part of a paragraph, but as a general rule you should not begin a sentence by referring to evidence, unless you go on in that sentence to explain the principle or idea to be discussed in the essay. You should tell the reader the point you are about to make before providing the evidence to back up that point. If you begin a sentence with a discussion of a case or a statute, then you are asking the reader to work out why it is important. It is similar to being in court as an advocate defending someone on trial for murder, standing up at the beginning of your submission to the jury and explaining that the police found a knife at the murder scene before proceeding to describe the knife in detail. If you then sat down, the jury would be left knowing a lot about a knife but without having any idea about how that helps your client's defence to the charge of murder. The jury have not been told the point of your exposition of the evidence and they could jump to any number of erroneous conclusions that do not help your argument in favour of your client. Instead, you need to explain the relevance of the knife to the jury in the hope that this will clear your client's name. Always explain your point first, then provide your evidence to prove your point.

Yet many of us find it almost impossible to begin our sentences with analysis and then to provide the evidence in support, instead we often begin by describing the evidence and then to grope our way towards our analysis by asking ourselves 'and so ... what ... in relation to the question?' Once we have the 'so what' we have our analysis, our conclusion. This approach is not problematic, but it does mean that we then need to redraft our sentences to take the analysis from the end, bring it to the beginning and then redraft the evidence so that it becomes the justification for our analysis rather than a description of what we read in the research phase. It may also lead us to combine sentences that were previously separate and to summarise our evidence further as follows:

Parliament is no longer supreme in the way that was envisaged by a traditional conception of parliamentary supremacy, since the UK became an EU member state. Parliament gave effect to EU law within the domestic jurisdiction and granted primacy to some forms of EU law in situations where there is a direct contradiction between UK law and EU law provisions, as indicated in its passing of the European Communities Act 1972, in particular section 2(1) of the Act, and as evidenced by judicial application of EU law in preference to contradictory domestic provisions in the case of *R v. Secretary of State for Transport ex p. Factortame (No. 2)* (1991). This suggests that the traditional conception of parliamentary supremacy requires some modification although given Parliament's continuing role in providing for EU law primacy it would not be accurate to say that Parliament had lost its supremacy entirely.

This is the reworked first sentence that takes into account what I have learned by the time I had finished drafting the paragraph for point 4 (see above)

This sentence amalgamates the four sentences that followed the first sentence in the earlier draft of the paragraph. It begins with analysis – my conclusion – and then justifies the conclusion with reference to the evidence (now summarised and used rather than simply described at length).

This is my new higher level conclusion having reread my paragraph and thought a little more about what this material means in the light of the question

A similar redrafting process is useful to improve the quality of each paragraph too. It is as well to redraft each paragraph once you have worked out your point (your conclusion on each issue) so as be sure that you are communicating your point from the beginning of the paragraph and also justifying it in the middle portion with reference to your evidence base. One easy way to do this is to take your concluding sentence from the end of your paragraph (assuming you have one!) and place it as the first sentence. Then redraft your discussion of the evidence to explain how it allowed you to reach this conclusion (what we shall now call your analysis). You may then want to reread the question, reread your paragraph again and then consider whether you are able to reach an even better conclusion that you can add to the end of the paragraph (critical analysis). As you will see in Chapter 7, you can repeat this redrafting cycle a number of times and thus repeatedly strengthen your analysis to improve the quality of your work. The aim is to make each sentence analytical – to explain your scholarly conclusions in each sentence – and to push up the quality of your analysis so that is becomes more and more sophisticated taking into account all the evidence that you have from your research phase. And that way your paragraphs should be full of critical analysis.

2.7: STAGE 6: THE CONCLUSION

- Draw the issues and their relevance together.

- Take the points that you have made at the end of each paragraph to construct your conclusion.

- Do not introduce new ideas.

Once you have exhausted all the issues on your list and provided evidence to back them up, you need to complete your essay by writing your conclusion. Your conclusion is the answer to the question in summary form, taking into account everything you have said previously in your answer. If you have followed the structure set out above then you should be able to read through the first and last sentences of each paragraph and pull those together into a conclusion to the question. Some people find it helpful to copy and paste these sentences into a single concluding paragraph, then redraft them as a coherent conclusion, reread the question, reread the concluding paragraph and then add their final thoughts, final analysis, to the end so as to round off the conclusion with higher level critical analysis.

I have mentioned description, analysis and critical analysis many times during this chapter, and it is often difficult for students to understand the difference particularly when they are told that their work is 'too descriptive', 'insufficiently analytical' or there is 'insufficient critical analysis'. I have given some guidance on this in the introduction chapter but the illustration on the next page may help to debunk the differences a little.

It is possible to use this writing and redrafting cycle to move from description, to analysis to critical analysis if you are willing to rework your essay through multiple drafts. At the note-taking stage you will describe what you have read (usually in summary form), at the planning stage you will begin to order that description into themes by pulling together notes from different sources and writing down what you think the theme is (its extent) and how it helps you with the question: this forms the early stages of analysis. You will refine your analysis as you write your paragraph, develop your conclusions to introduce your paragraph, discuss how your evidence has led you to those conclusions. As you redraft the paragraph and the essay again and again and reach higher level conclusions that take into account all the evidence that you have found then your analysis will develop to a higher level of critique, as it develops across paragraphs and not just within paragraphs.

But even at this stage you have not completed your conclusion and your essay. Double-check that you have not introduced new material into your conclusion that begs new questions that should have been answered in your essay already. Further, ensure that your conclusion accords with the rest of your essay; in other words, do not tack on a conclusion that you think the marker will agree with even though your essay is pointing in a totally different direction. There are rarely right and wrong answers in essays and it is better to write a conclusion that fits with your essay than to manufacture a conclusion that you think will be popular. And now that you know what your conclusions are you should work your way back through your essay slowly, making amendments as you go so as to integrate your conclusions throughout it. Then move on to check that you have properly referenced your work (see Chapter 6); and review the chapter on finishing and polishing (Chapter 7) as formatting, presentation, proofreading and redrafting can all contribute to a stronger mark. Also double-check that you are within the word count, and have met the deadline and any other assessment requirements. You may also want to revisit feedback from previous essays (including ones for other subjects) to make sure that you have built on your strengths and not replicated previous errors.

Dissect the question into sub-questions, develop keywords for research phase. Make a note of your understanding of the question to help with this part of the introduction.

Locating and Marshalling Material
Use keywords to locate relevant sources. Sort sources into piles:
a   Directly relevant to the question
b   Relevant to some but not all aspects of the question
c   Not now sure how relevant

Submit!

Reading and Descriptive Note-taking 1
Read each group 'a' source, describe (note) succinctly ideas relevant to the question. Note the full citation for each.

Final Approach
Run through the finishing and polishing stages.

Reading and Descriptive Note-taking 2
Read each group 'b' source, describe (note) succinctly ideas relevant to the question. Note the full citation for each. Skim through the group 'c' sources and note any relevant material too.

Pre-final Draft
Reread your draft, consider whether it fully answers the question. Do you need more research to fill in any gaps, make any justifications more persuasive, etc.?

Organising and Imposing Structure – Analytical Thinking
Read your notes, jot down any repeated themes/issues. Reorganise your notes under these theme headings. Set out these themes in the draft introduction, to act as a signpost to what will follow in your essay.

Developing Critical Analysis
Reread your whole draft slowly and redraft so as to integrate what you have learned so far. Consider taking the conclusions from the bottom of each paragraph to the top, redrafting the justification in the middle to reflect your new understanding, look back at the question, reread each paragraph and add a new higher level conclusion to the end. Repeat this process as many times as you can.

Developing Persuasive Writing
Take each theme in turn, read your notes, jot down how your notes help you to answer the question. Place this conclusion sentence at the top of the paragraph, redraft the notes that follow to show how your research evidence has helped you to reach that conclusion. Repeat for each theme.

Developing Critical Conclusions
Take your conclusions from each paragraph to form the first draft of your overarching conclusion, reread the question and reread the conclusion and add a couple of sentences of overview conclusion as a final answer to the question.

Developing More Sophisticated, Persuasive Analysis
Reread each draft paragraph and reflect on what it means in the context of the question. Add this higher level conclusion to the bottom of your paragraph. Make any additional amendments to the paragraph.

Next steps:

You may wish to look back through a previous essay that you have written in the light of what you have just read, then look again at Chapter 1 and consider too the guidance on feedback provided in Chapter 9. What positives and negatives can you spot in your essay that you did not necessarily spot at the time? What about the feedback that you received: does that accord with your new understandings; can you learn from it for your next essay; would it help you to rework one or two of those paragraphs according to the guidance in this chapter and then ask for further feedback from your tutor?

You may wish to find an example of an essay question, either from one of your course or module handbooks or from a past exam paper.

1 Read the question and dissect it. Do you understand exactly what the question is asking?

2 Read through your lecture and tutorial notes for the topic that forms the basis of the essay. What are the key issues that are pertinent to the question? List them.

3 Write a sentence after each of the key issues, summarising what it is.

4 Note down any evidence that you have in support or against each of these issues.

5 Consider how each of the key issues may help you to answer the question and write that underneath it.

6 Consider where you would go to find other evidence, were you to attempt to write a full answer to this question.

7 Then consider how confident you now feel at answering that question. Does this technique help you to focus on the task? How would you refine it for future essays?

You may now wish to try and test your knowledge of essay writing and compare your paragraphs against those at the end of the book, in addition to working your way through the additional exercises on the companion website.

Q TEST YOUR KNOWLEDGE OF ESSAY WRITING

- Have a go at writing an introduction, a middle paragraph or two middle paragraphs of your own, for the essay title used as an example above:

'The British Parliament was once supreme.' Discuss with reference to Britain's membership of the EU and its obligations in relation to the European Convention on Human Rights.

- Consider your paragraph structure. Does your paragraph begin with a sentence or sentences setting out the issue to be discussed, a middle section in which the discussion takes place, and a concluding sentence or sentences in which the issues within the paragraph are explained in the light of the question?

- You may wish to compare your paragraphs against those in the answer section towards the end of the book, and also to good, and not so good, examples on the companion website.

 Visit the companion website for examples of good and bad practice.

SUMMARY

You may find the following essay writing stages assist you in writing essays. Do not begin these stages until you have completed those set out in Chapter 1.

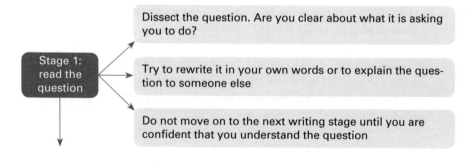

Stage 1: read the question

Dissect the question. Are you clear about what it is asking you to do?

Try to rewrite it in your own words or to explain the question to someone else

Do not move on to the next writing stage until you are confident that you understand the question

Stage 2: read through your notes and make a list of relevant issues

Read through your lecture notes on the topics covered by the question

Read through your tutorial notes on the topics covered by the question

Undertake further research in books, journals, cases and legislative sources and make notes on issues relevant to the question

Stage 3: organise your ideas into a logical order

Read through your notes and group similar issues together. These will become your themes/ideas. Write a sentence after each idea to explain how it relates to the question

Number the themes/ideas in an order that appears to be logical to develop your arguments

Note down the evidence you have for each theme/idea, in terms of cases, legislation, quotes, etc.

You are now ready to start writing

Stage 4: write the introduction

Briefly explain the task that you are undertaking. You may wish to use the text of the question that you rewrote at an earlier stage

Set out the issues that you will deal with in your essay and how you will approach the question

Stage 5: write the middle section of the essay

Organise your ideas into paragraphs. One paragraph should contain one issue

Begin each paragraph by stating the point that will be discussed within it

Discuss the point in the middle section of the paragraph

Use evidence to back up your points. Does each point have evidence that supports it?

Conclude each paragraph by explaining what the point means in relation to the question

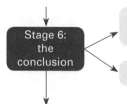

Stage 6:
the
conclusion

Draw the issues and their relevance together to provide a final answer to the question

Do not introduce new ideas into the conclusion

Move on to the finishing, polishing stages and check that all references to others' work are full and accurate (these stages are discussed in subsequent chapters)

3

ANSWERING PROBLEM QUESTIONS

Problem questions are vignettes – scenes set out for you to jump into and legal problems for you to diagnose. They are a form of role play and can be quite fun if you approach them in the correct way. They are similar to essay answers in some ways; however, they are designed to test some different skills. Problem questions focus on a student's ability to diagnose the legal problem, to apply the law to the facts in the problem and to provide accurate advice on the likely chances of success if a case were to be taken further. They also test the ability to argue competing precedents, by arguing cases for and against the party to be advised. They consider how well a student can provide alternative courses of action to the client and identify issues that may need further investigation before full advice can be given. This chapter will take a scenario that is public law-based, and follow it through the process. There is a further and different example on the companion website, should you require more guidance.

3.1: STAGE 1: READ THE SCENARIO CAREFULLY

- Read the scenario carefully.

- Read it again.

- Make a list of facts and put them in chronological order.

We will work through the problem question set out in the introduction, to consider how best to approach writing an answer to a factual scenario. There are many ways to approach problem question answers; this is by no means the only way to diagnose the legal problem and to write an opinion on the legal options open to the party to be advised. However, if you are unsure about how to approach problem questions, this may be a good way to start the process.

The scenario is as follows:

Parliament has introduced a new licensing scheme to make sure that all individuals who want to work as art dealers must hold a licence. Parliament passes the Art Dealers Licensing Act 2015 and the Act states that the new Licensing Authority is responsible for administering the Art Dealers' licensing scheme. Section 2 states that 'The Licensing Authority may issue a licence to an individual to act as an art dealer if the individual has not been convicted of a serious criminal offence and if the individual has a recognised qualification in an art-related subject'. The Act further states that a degree in art or art history from a UK university will automatically be recognised for the purposes of the Act. Interim arrangements exist which require current art dealers to apply for a licence within six months of entry into force of the Act.

The following events occur:
Ruth works for an art dealer in London. Ruth is not sure whether she needs a licence as she currently does not sell art, she only values it. She has no criminal convictions and has a degree in art history from a UK university. She applies to the Licensing Authority for a licence, just in case she needs to have one. Her application is refused. The Authority writes to tell her that she must stop her work immediately as she does not have the required qualification and she is not a fit and proper person to be an art dealer. In the letter the Authority tells her that the decision is final and cannot be challenged in any court whatsoever. Ruth telephones the Licensing Authority to see whether she really needs a licence and speaks to John, the decision-maker. In the course of the conversation he lets slip that he considers that women do not make good art dealers or valuers. Ruth seeks legal advice from you.

The professional publication for art dealers runs an article in their journal about Ruth's situation. A reader of the publication, Phillip, hears of the problem and approaches Ruth to let her know that he would be willing to challenge the decision on her behalf as he is a dealer who has female employees working for him and he is scandalised by what he has heard of her case.

Advise Ruth about her case and Phillip's suggestion to her about his role in bringing an action on her behalf.

Problem questions are relatively easy to approach, although the law that you need to apply may be complicated. First, read the scenario – obvious, yes, but it is tempting to jump in when you recognise something that you think you can write about. Next, read it again. You will not pick up on all the facts and the importance of the facts on the first reading. You may find it useful to write a list of events in chronological order, or, if you prefer, to draw a diagram showing who did what to whom, when and apparently why.

1   Ruth works for an art dealer but is not currently an art dealer herself; she is an art valuer.

2   The Art Dealers' Licensing Scheme is introduced requiring all art dealers to have a licence in order to practise as art dealers.

3   Ruth applies to the Licensing Authority for a licence under the Art Dealers' Licensing Scheme.

4   Ruth applies on the basis that she has a degree in Art History from a recognised university and she has no criminal convictions, in keeping with the requirements of the Act. She appears to have met the requirements for a licence.

5   The Authority refuses Ruth's licence.

6   Ruth is told that she must stop working in her current job as she does not have a licence. She is told that the decision is final.

7   Ruth telephones the Authority and she claims that during that conversation the decision-maker tells her that he does not believe women make good art dealers or valuers.

8   Ruth wants to challenge the decision.

9   Phillip reads about Ruth's situation in the trade press and wants to challenge the decision on her behalf through the courts.

10   I have been asked to provide legal advice for Ruth.

Hopefully by now you will have a good factual basis from which to work. Make sure that you identify for whom you are working; in other words, who is the client seeking advice and what are they hoping to achieve if they have given an indication of the outcome they hope for. This will be important once you come to write up your opinion and it may also help you to bear this in mind when you are trying to work out the legal basis of the case. This is the factual analysis of the problem.

3.2: STAGE 2: FACTUAL ANALYSIS

- Consider which of the facts are agreed.

- Consider which facts are or may be disputed.

- Are there any facts that you need but have not been given?

Consider which of the facts are agreed. In other words, which facts can you rely on as both sides share the same view of what happened? Which facts are disputed? In other words, where is there a difference of opinion about the facts? These will need to be argued in your answer. Are there any facts that you require but have not been given? You will need to say this in your answer to show that the solicitor or the direct individual client will need to investigate these areas further, before you can provide a final opinion.

1 Ruth works for an art dealer but is not currently an art dealer herself; she is an art valuer. – Not sure whether the Licensing Authority agrees that she is a valuer rather than a dealer.

2 The Art Dealers' Licensing Scheme is introduced requiring all art dealers to have a licence in order to practise as art dealers. – Agreed.

3 Ruth applies to the local authority for a licence under the Art Dealers' Licensing Scheme. – Agreed.

4 Ruth applies on the basis that she has a degree in Art History from a recognised university and she has no criminal convictions, in keeping with the requirements of the Act. – Disagreement. She believes she meets the requirements; the Authority appears to believe she does not.

5 The Authority refuses Ruth's licence. – Agreed.

6 Ruth is told that she must stop working in her current job as she does not have a licence. She is told that the decision is final. – Agreed, factually, but Ruth believes that the decision is wrong and should be capable of challenge.

7 Ruth telephones the Licensing Authority and the decision-maker tells her that he does not believe women make good art dealers or valuers. – Not sure whether this is agreed with the Authority. The decision-maker may dispute this comment.

8 Ruth wants to challenge the decision. – Current position.

9 Phillip reads about Ruth's situation in the trade press and wants to challenge the decision on her behalf through the courts. – Current position.

10 I have been asked to provide legal advice to Ruth on her case and on the extent to which Phillip may bring a case on her behalf. – Current position.

This serves as a means to identify which legal principles you may need to refer to/research and which areas are contested (and thus will need to be examined in detail) and those which are agreed and may be addressed in less detail assuming the law is relatively clear on each point.

3.3:   STAGE 3: RESEARCH AND LEGAL ANALYSIS

> ● **Consider which area of law is the subject of the problem.**
>
> ● **Look at the key concepts for that area of law and consider which may apply to the clients' situations.**
>
> ● **List any tests that have to be considered for each of the concepts.**
>
> ● **Plan your answer.**

The next step is to work out the legal areas that are relevant to the case. First pinpoint the subject area. You will probably have been given the problem question in a particular subject, for example public law. Next try to work out the topic areas that are relevant to the problem. What do the facts suggest? Look back through your notes if you are not sure; the chances are that you have been lectured on the area already, or you will have been assigned reading to do in preparation for the problem. Once you have decided upon the topics that are relevant, reread your notes, then reread the problem. Finally extract the relevant issues from the notes you have from your lectures, tutorials and reading. Some guidance is provided on the companion website, including examples of how you may make use of authority in this context.

You will then need to undertake additional research so that you have a good grounding in the legal principles (the cases and legislation) and have authority or authoritative evidence that you may use as the basis to develop your understanding of your client's case, then to develop your analysis of the strength of their case, and then to write your legal opinion so as to justify your analysis. You cannot write a strong problem question answer without reference to case law and legislation, and without explaining explicitly how the specific points of law relate to the facts of your client's case and thus what is your analysis of the client's case. You may need to quote case law and statutory references and explain how that wording and reasoning has led you to your conclusion on each point of law. If you are unsure how to conduct your research then please refer to Chapter 5, and to Chapter 6 if you need assistance with how to quote or paraphrase your sources and to cite them.

Visit the companion website at www.routledge.com/cw/webley for further guidance.

A broad outline of the legal area would look something like this:

Area of Law – public law case – judicial review according to Civil Procedure Rules Part 54.

Necessary requirements for a judicial review to be sought:

1. *Decision-maker must be a public body. Is it? Public functions test? See* ex parte Datafin *(1987) and* ex parte Agha Khan *(1983).*
2. *Clients must have standing – sufficient interest test s 31(3) Senior Court Act 1981. Do Ruth and Phillip have standing under the sufficient interest test?*
3. *Judicial review must be brought within the time limit – no suggestion that out of time, but we need to be aware of the time limit and advise the client accordingly.*
4. *Relevance of the comment in the letter stating that she cannot challenge the decision in court? Is there an ouster clause in the Act? Does not appear so and in any event, see* Anisminic. *It looks as though there is no reason why the court would consider this issue non-justiciable.*
5. *Client's advocate must be able to argue at least one ground for judicial review – illegality, irrationality and procedural impropriety, including the rules of natural justice. Illegality and irrationality. Does not appear to be a procedural impropriety.*
6. *Client is seeking a remedy through judicial review – consider the range of remedies available.*
7. *Conclude by stating Ruth's chances of success and possible remedies and Phillip's chance of being permitted to bring the action on behalf of Ruth.*

You may now begin to plan your answer in a similar way to the way that you would plan an essay, as discussed in the previous chapter. You should plan your answer by splitting up the issues in the same way as you would for an essay; in other words to assign one paragraph per issue or point and to plan each paragraph individually. To begin with you may begin each paragraph by explaining the issue to be discussed, and after your answer has gone through a couple of drafts it may begin with your explanation of the conclusion that you have reached on the issue. At first draft stage the middle section of the paragraph may contain a more developed discussion of the issue, with evidence to back up the points being made. At a later stage the middle section may be by way of a justification for your analysis (the conclusion you have reached on the issue) in which you explain exactly how the evidence supports your analysis rather than describing the evidence that you have found. The paragraph would often conclude by explaining clearly what the legal issue means as regards the client's case, in this instance for Ruth and for Phillip. You may wish to refresh your memory of how to plan and structure a paragraph by reviewing the relevant section of Chapter 2.

3.4: STAGE 4: INTRODUCTION

- Explain the basic situation, briefly, and who you have been asked to advise.

- Set out the issues upon which you will give a legal opinion.

Problem question answers can be difficult to begin to write, because it is hard to know how to start off your answer. The simplest way to open your answer is to set out who you are advising and the nature of the case. Try to avoid reiterating all the facts in detail, as it will take too long and is unnecessary, as the client and the solicitor will already know the facts of the case. Some markers will prefer you not to explain the facts other than when they are relevant to the legal point that you are making. Do check this with your tutor if you are unsure of current practice in your law school. An example of an introduction for the problem question would be as follows:

This sentence sets out the parties to be advised and the body against which an action will be sought

The sentence also identifies that the Licensing Authority must be a public body, which is a necessary condition for a judicial review action

This demonstrates the need for standing

In order to consider the merits of Ruth's case and to advise her (and Phillip) accordingly, it is important to establish whether the Licensing Body, the body that made the decision to refuse her a licence, is a public body susceptible to judicial review. In addition, it is necessary to consider whether Ruth and Phillip have standing to bring a judicial review case. The decision will be examined for elements of illegality, irrationality and procedural impropriety. Finally, the client will be advised on potential remedies.

The third sentence sets out the substantive grounds to be considered

The final sentence states that the client will be advised on the strength of her case

This is likely to be refined once you have reached firm conclusions in respect of the problem, and you may wish to provide a summary of your findings, your conclusions, in the introduction once you are clear on what they are.

You may wish to approach your problem question answer in a similar way to the structure set out in Chapter 2 for essay answers, until you feel more confident, so as to develop your own approach and style (including leaving your introduction until you have written the first draft of the main body of your answer). However, there are a few differences between essays and problem question answers. Problem answers deal with a set of facts and provide a legal assessment based on those facts. It is important that you know what you need to prove or disprove in order to provide an assessment of your client's chances of success, if the case were to go to court or were to be settled on the basis of legal norms. If you are not able to put down the points that you need to establish then you are not yet clear on the law in the area. Return to your notes to work out what must be established in order to show that a contract has been established, or that the offence of theft has been committed or that a client is able to challenge a decision through judicial review.

From then on, until your conclusion, each issue should be discussed in turn in a separate paragraph. Look back at your introduction – what issues did you say you had to establish? Assign each issue one paragraph. Then plan the rest of your answer as follows:

3.5: ISSUE ONE ON YOUR LIST

- Write down the issue to be discussed.

- What do you need to establish to show that this issue has been proved or disproved?

- What evidence do you have to elaborate or to support these points in legal terms? Are there cases that are evidence for the general principles? Are there statutory extracts that are of relevance? Are there quotes or comments from academic texts that assist?

- Why is this issue relevant to the client and what does this mean in relation to the client's case?

All you then need to do is to write up that paragraph, but in order to do so you may need to undertake some research and employ your legal skills so as to analyse legislation and case law. The simplest way to make a start at writing is to follow the paragraph plan described in the Chapter 2, on essay writing. Your first sentence should set out the point you will deal with in your answer. This will be a description of issue one you highlighted in your planning stage:

> It is important to consider whether Ruth is able to establish that the Licensing Authority that refused her a licence is a public body, because public bodies may be judicially reviewed whereas most private bodies may not.

Or something along those lines.

Your next few sentences – the middle part of your paragraph – will at first draft stage take the reader through the principles that must be proved in order to establish whether or not, in this instance, the body is a public body. You should have evidence to back up every point you make. Evidence may be in the form of a case that establishes the test for what constitutes a public body – evidence could be a reference to a statute that sets out a test. Your evidence may even be in the form of academic opinion from a book or a journal article. You should be able to point to something that confirms what you are saying and it is important to back up your points; otherwise, as a barrister, you are saying to the solicitor 'this is true because I say so' (which generally is not going to be enough, and certainly could land you in very hot water if your advice is later found to be wrong!). In later drafts it should be possible for you to explain how your evidence (usually cases and legislation in this context) justifies the conclusion that you have reached as regards this legal point given how the law applies to the facts. In other words, in later drafts you will combine what you have worked out with the evidence that led you to that conclusion, that analysis, rather than having a sentence in which you describe your evidence followed by a sentence in which you explain your conclusion.

> Ruth must establish that the body in question is a public body in order to mount a challenge to the decision through judicial review. The decision-making body is the Licensing Authority, which is exercising powers that have been conferred on it by statute and is administering a statutory licensing scheme. Its power is public in nature, similar to the power exercised by the Takeover and Mergers Panel in the case of R v. City Panel on Takeovers and Mergers ex parte Datafin Ltd [1987] QB 815 in which Lloyd LJ stated: 'if a body in question is exercising public law functions, or if the exercise of its functions has public law consequences, then that may be sufficient to bring the body within the reach of judicial review.'[1]

1 H. Barnett, *Constitutional and Administrative Law* (11th edn, Routledge-Cavendish, 2015) p. 607.

You may be able to provide more case law in support of this proposition. One case is a good start, but there are others that you could use to reinforce the point or to refine it. And although you may well have read about the case in the textbook (and so you must reference the textbook) it is better to read the case in its original form via the law reports.

Even then, this is only two-thirds of the paragraph, even though many students move on to the next point at this stage and by doing so lose vital marks. You now need to apply the law to Ruth's situation. So far you have given general advice on the law in the area and this is not much use to Ruth, who does not want to pay for a law lecture. The next stage, which will push you up to the next level of marks, is to say what the law means to Ruth. This is more straightforward than students think. All you need to do is to quickly reread what you have written, look again at your list or diagram of the facts that you drew up earlier on, and write a few sentences on how and why the law as discussed is relevant to Ruth. Does this mean she is in a strong legal position on this point, or a weaker position? Does this mean that she should be advised to take an action if the other side will not agree to her terms, or should she seek a different course of action? Your last sentence, thus, rounds off the point:

> *Consequently, the Licensing Authority's decision is susceptible to judicial review.*

Once you have completed this stage in the paragraph you may want to redraft the paragraph so as to develop your analysis in the paragraph. To do this you will take what you now know, that the licensing authority is a public body, and begin your paragraph on that basis:

> *Decisions made by the Licensing Authority, such as the decision made in respect of Ruth's application for a licence, are open to challenge via judicial review. The Licensing Authority is classed as a public body as it is exercising powers that have been conferred on it by statute and it is administering a statutory licensing scheme. Consequently its power is public in nature, similar to the power exercised by the Takeover and Mergers Panel in the case of R v. City Panel on Takeovers and Mergers ex parte Datafin Ltd [1987] QB 815 in which Lloyd LJ stated: 'if a body in question is exercising public law functions, or if the exercise of its functions has public law consequences, then that may be sufficient to bring the body within the reach of judicial review.'[1] Consequently were we to challenge the decision through the courts we would use the judicial review jurisdiction to do so.*

1 H. Barnett, *Constitutional and Administrative Law* (11th edn, Routledge, 2015) p. 607.

It is difficult to develop this paragraph much further without greater evidence to assist us in our analysis development and our critique. And so further research would be beneficial to help us to provide a more sophisticated assessment on this particular point. However, the paragraph has at least been redrafted so as to set out the conclusion at the start, and to explain its relevance at the end. And the evidence has been explained in the light of Ruth's situation rather than described first and then analysed second. This has allowed for an additional conclusion (an additional piece of analysis) to be generated and at the end of the paragraph too.

You are now ready to move on to a new paragraph to discuss the next issue on your list in the same terms. Once you have exhausted all the issues on the list, go back to the problem question. Is there anything in there that you have missed? Have you exhausted all the legal issues suggested by the facts? If not then continue with the paragraph system. Check your notes on the topic to be sure that there are no other issues that could be relevant to Ruth's case or to Phillip, who also wishes to challenge the decision. If so then you are ready to move on to the conclusion.

3.6: Why Use Evidence?

> **Do not make a statement unless you can back it up with evidence.**
>
> **Evidence could be (for example):**
>
> - judicial opinion from a case;
>
> - sections from a statute;
>
> - views of a commentator: an academic or practitioner, or another relevant spokesperson.

3.6.1 HOW DO I USE EVIDENCE?

Evidence is just as it sounds – something to back up a point that you are making. Evidence is never a point in itself and consequently you should not begin a paragraph by setting out your evidence. Instead, you need to explain what point you are going to make, then provide the evidence to show that what you say is true. You should try to avoid the following, in which a student has put the cart before the horse, the evidence before the point:

> In the case of *Anisminic v. Foreign Compensation Commission* [1969] 2 AC 147 the court held that errors of law may be reviewable in circumstances in which an ouster clause would ordinarily oust the jurisdiction of the court.

This could be simply rephrased to look something like this:

This sentence introduces the issue to be discussed	The second sentence provides relevant background to the issues

Ruth has to establish whether the comment made in the letter, which suggests that the Licensing Authority's decision could not be reviewed by a court, is backed up by an ouster clause in the relevant statute. An ouster clause is a provision in an Act which ousts, or removes, the jurisdiction of the court in relation to any decision or action taken under the authority of the Act. There does not appear to be such a clause in the Act, but this will require further investigation. In addition, there is judicial evidence to suggest that an ouster clause may not entirely remove the court's jurisdiction, even if one were present in the Act. The case of *Anisminic v. Foreign Compensation Commission* [1969] 2 AC 147 establishes that where there is an imputation of an error of law, the court will see past the ouster clause to consider whether an illegality has been committed by the decision-maker. This will override the ouster clause and permit the judicial review to be heard. On this basis there is no reason to suspect that the Licensing Authority is correct in its suggestion the decision is unchallengeable.

This relates the issue to the question and suggests the need for further investigation of the facts

This applies the law to the facts

This provides evidence in support of the legal principle

The final sentence provides a conclusion to the issue

A case has been used as evidence in this paragraph, but statutory references should be treated in the same way. They should be used as evidence of what the law is rather than to back up a point you are making. Quotes from academic texts are to be used similarly, as are those from other sources. Note that you do not always need to quote the works in a case, statute or academic text; it may be better to paraphrase the relevant points, but do always cite your sources. You may wish to review the material in Chapter 6 on quoting, paraphrasing and citing your sources, and there is additional material on the companion website. It may also help to read Chapter 5, which gives advice on how to make use of evidence in your writing.

At this stage, you will need to review your paragraph structure, as discussed in Chapter 2. Each problem question answer will go through a number of drafts so as to develop the analysis and strengthen the justification for that analysis with reference to your evidence base. You may wish to try the technique suggested in the previous chapter, namely to take the conclusion that you have reached at the end of each paragraph, place it at the beginning of the paragraph, redraft the middle section as a justification for how the evidence supports your analysis and then consider whether you are able to reach an even higher level conclusion to add at the end. We worked through this technique in 3.5 above, to demonstrate how to move from description with analysis to more developed analysis.

3.7: CONCLUSION

> - **Pull together all the legal evidence to provide an assessment of the strengths and weaknesses of the client's case.**
>
> - **Provide the options open to the client.**
>
> - **State any further investigation that may need to be undertaken prior to a final opinion being reached (if there are factual gaps or inconsistencies).**

The conclusion should summarise the strengths and weaknesses of the client's case and suggest the likely outcome if their case were to be adjudicated. In addition, the conclusion may provide an assessment of the ways to settle the case using negotiation, mediation and arbitration. It may also set out any avenues that the solicitor will need to explore, before a final legal opinion may be given, for example any factual inconsistencies that may have a bearing on the case. The conclusion should not leave the solicitor or his or her client with unanswered legal questions.

Your conclusion should be one paragraph in which you provide your assessment of the client's chances of success if the case were to come to court, and it should also address remedies and/or the likely outcome. If you have followed the paragraph formula above it may be possible for you to read through the first and the last few lines of each paragraph and, by pulling all of those together, show the strengths and weaknesses of your client's case. This determines what advice you would give to your client as far as adjudication, mediation, settlement or other action is concerned. If your case is one for which the client may be entitled to damages, and you have not dealt with issues of quantum (level of damages) in your classes, then it is unlikely that your tutor will expect you to predict the amount of money the client would win. That said, you should be able to make a judgement on whether the client has a strong or a weak case and what they would be asking for if there are alternative remedies open to them. In a criminal case you would be giving an assessment of whether the client is likely to be found guilty, unless you have been asked to advise on other issues such as defences, for example.

Now that you are clear on your conclusions you need to begin at the beginning of your answer so as to redraft it knowing what you now know. This will help you to develop your analysis between paragraphs and not just within paragraphs, and thus it will also help you to add critique. There may be alternative options open to the client (some grounds may be stronger than others) and you can signpost this within the paragraphs rather than leaving it until the final conclusion. There may be links to be made across paragraphs, for example by arguing one point you may need to forgo another point as it may not be possible to argue both alternatives successfully. Continue to redraft, or tweak, your answer until you find that you are not able to come up with any new insights as you read through it. Finally, you need to reread and polish your written work. Further guidance on this stage can be found in Chapter 7.

This chapter has shown that problem questions are relatively straightforward to write as long as you split the process up into small sections. Each paragraph is a self-contained unit, which sets out an issue, discusses the issue with evidence to back up the points that are made, and then concludes with an explanation of the relevance of the issue to the question. By building up the essay or problem question answer through single paragraphs, your answer should be well structured, clear and evidenced.

Next steps:

Now that you have read through the chapter you may want to review one of your own problem question answers.

1 **First take a problem question that you have already attempted and carry out a factual analysis.**

2 **Carry out a legal analysis including research if necessary.**

3 **Read back through your problem question answer. Did you identify the pertinent facts and legal issues?**

4 **Looking at your answer, did you deal with each legal issue in a separate paragraph?**

5 **Did you introduce each issue, discuss its relevance with the aid of authoritative evidence and provide an assessment of how that legal issue would be decided in your client's case?**

6 Did you address all the legal issues that were relevant to your client's case?

7 Did you provide a conclusion setting out the likely chances of success were the client to go to court?

Now consider how you could improve your answer. Reread any feedback you have previously been given and see whether you understand better what was said. You may want to refresh your memory of how you are assessed, in Chapter 1, and refer to the Chapter 9 on how to make the most of feedback too.

You may wish to visit the companion website for examples of good and less good problem question paragraphs.

You may also wish to compare this way of approaching problem question answers with the CLEO method (claim, law, evaluation, outcome). A good book to read on this is S.I. Strong, *How to Write Law Essays and Exams* 4th edn (Oxford: Oxford University Press, 2014).

Now visit www.routledge.com/cw/webley for more problem questions and answers.

SUMMARY

The following stages may assist in approaching, structuring and writing answers to problem questions.

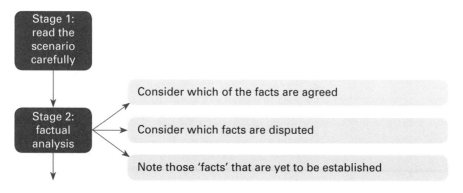

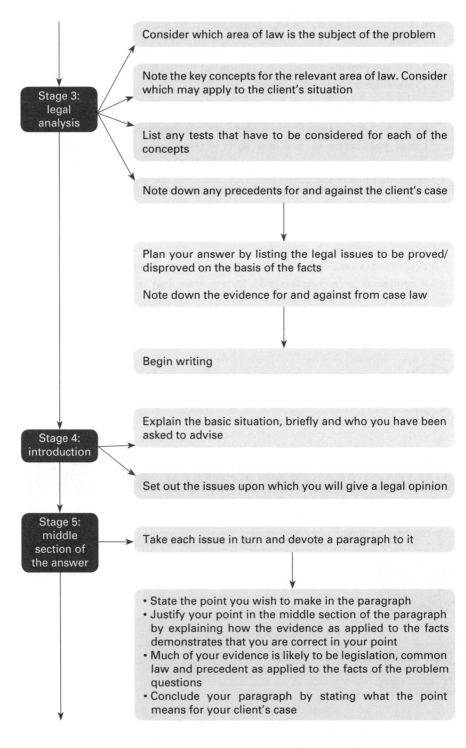

Consider which area of law is the subject of the problem

Stage 3: legal analysis

Note the key concepts for the relevant area of law. Consider which may apply to the client's situation

List any tests that have to be considered for each of the concepts

Note down any precedents for and against the client's case

Plan your answer by listing the legal issues to be proved/ disproved on the basis of the facts

Note down the evidence for and against from case law

Begin writing

Stage 4: introduction

Explain the basic situation, briefly and who you have been asked to advise

Set out the issues upon which you will give a legal opinion

Stage 5: middle section of the answer

Take each issue in turn and devote a paragraph to it

• State the point you wish to make in the paragraph
• Justify your point in the middle section of the paragraph by explaining how the evidence as applied to the facts demonstrates that you are correct in your point
• Much of your evidence is likely to be legislation, common law and precedent as applied to the facts of the problem questions
• Conclude your paragraph by stating what the point means for your client's case

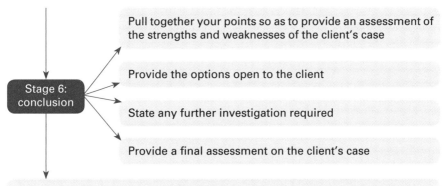

Pull together your points so as to provide an assessment of the strengths and weaknesses of the client's case

Provide the options open to the client

Stage 6: conclusion

State any further investigation required

Provide a final assessment on the client's case

Move on to the finishing, polishing stages and check that all references to others' work are full and accurate (these stages are discussed in subsequent chapters)

Q TEST YOUR KNOWLEDGE OF ESSAY WRITING

Review a paragraph you have written previously for a problem question answer. Consider your paragraph structure. Does your paragraph:

- begin with a sentence or sentences setting out the legal point that you have identified as pertinent to your client's case;
- contain a middle section in which you explain how the legal principle applies in this instance with reference to the case law and/or legislation and how that justifies your legal advice;
- lead to a concluding sentence that explains the relevance or importance of this legal point as regards your client's case?

What amendments, if any, would you make to your problem question answer, in the light of what you have learnt?

You may wish to compare your paragraphs against those in the answer section towards the end of the book, and also to good, and not so good, examples on the companion website.

4 WRITING EXTENDED ESSAYS AND DISSERTATIONS

Extended essays and dissertations are very similar to standard essays in many respects; however, the depth and range of research is more extensive than for a 2,500-word piece of coursework. There are some differences, which relate to the way in which one constructs a question to form the basis for your study, and the way in which one sets about undertaking the study that will result in the dissertation. This chapter considers one way to approach dissertation writing, although there are many others; feel free to depart from the approach adopted in this chapter once you feel confident in your ability to set a question, undertake a study and write up your findings in an academic manner.

4.1: Stage 1: Establish the Topic Upon Which You Wish to Write

- **Find a topic that is of interest to you.**

- **Read around the topic.**

- **Consider the sources available to you in the library.**

- **Discuss the topic with your supervisor.**

- **Finalise the topic upon which you wish to write.**

The earlier that you can set your topic the better for your later research; much time can be wasted by swapping topics from one week to the next. However, it is important to know that the topic is of interest to you and also that there are sources available in the library to assist you if you are planning to undertake library-based research. You also need to make sure that your topic is one with which your supervisor is familiar and so you should choose your topic carefully and in conjunction with your supervisor.

4.2: STAGE 2: NARROW DOWN THE TOPIC

> - **The topic is likely to be far too wide to form the basis of a dissertation.**
> - **You will need to narrow down the topic to a specific aspect of the topic.**
> - **The more specific you can be, the easier it will be to research.**

Students usually choose very wide topics upon which to write. This is, in part, a function of a lack of detailed knowledge in the area, a concern that a dissertation is an extended piece of writing and the idea that the topic must be wide enough to allow a student to write 10,000 words or more. It is also, in part, the fact that it is hard to be specific in the early stages of any research project. It is, perhaps, helpful to consider a dissertation as a research project and the writing part of the dissertation as the phase(s) in which you work out what are your research findings and what is their importance so as to report them to the reader. It is easier to undertake a project if you are clear on its parameters. The narrower the topic, the easier it is to research and also the easier it will be to show a depth of knowledge and analysis. Dissertations on broad topics tend to suffer from too much description – there is, after all, a lot to describe – and insufficient analysis and depth. It is as if one can either go broad and along the surface or narrow and deep. The narrower the topic, the easier it is to demonstrate depth and thus to achieve higher marks.

4.3: STAGE 3: TURN THE TOPIC OR STATEMENT INTO A QUESTION

> - **It is easier to undertake a research project in response to a question than a topic or statement.**
> - **Rephrase the dissertation statement as a question.**

Dissertation modules often require students to come up with a research topic, a research question and then a dissertation that answers that research question. This is a departure from many other forms of legal writing, as for most assessments a lecturer will have set you a question rather than you having to develop your own. A dissertation is an enquiry to answer a question; it is not a discussion of a topic in general terms. It will be easier to focus your research and your writing on achieving your goal (a well-researched and presented extended piece of critical analysis for which you will receive a high mark) if you set a question early on in the process. It may be helpful for you to talk to your supervisor about which aspects of the topic you are interested in, and during that process try to come up with a broad question that encompasses your discussions, but which is sufficiently certain and discrete that it is capable of answer within your time period (usually two terms). Many students find it helpful to begin the question with 'To what extent...?' followed by the kernel of the question that piques your interest. For example:

> Dissertation question: To what extent does the UK comply with the European Convention on Human Rights with respect to balancing article 10 (freedom of expression) with article 8 (the right to a private and family life) when questions of privacy versus newspapers' right to publish a story come into conflict?

Formulating a question may help you to write a dissertation proposal (if one is required) whereby you set out your topic, your research question, what interests you about the question (why this research question?), a bit of background about your study, and how you will seek to answer the question. Further, and throughout your study, the question affords you the opportunity of first describing what you have found through research and reading, then developing analysis (through reordering of material into themes and considerations of the links between the themes and the question and between the themes themselves) and then critical analysis as you deepen your critique of your evidence and also your initial analysis to reach even higher levels of nuanced and sophisticated analysis.

A note of caution is probably needed at this stage. If you think you have the answer to your question already in mind, then be honest about this and put this down on paper as a hypothesis – a proposition that you pose and which you then subject to research analysis in order to discover the extent to which you are right. A dissertation is not an exercise in proving your initial point or view; it is a process of enquiry to allow you to reach a considered decision on your question. However, if you do have an initial impression it is important to recognise this and to challenge it rather than to pretend you are open to all viewpoints when really you are trying to fit the evidence you find to the answer you want to provide in your writing. One-sided analysis is of poor quality and this will be reflected in the eventual mark you receive. And often your marker will have read more widely on the topic than you will have done and so s/he will spot that you have selected only the sources that appeal to your own biases – we all have them, but we need to recognise them and seek to challenge them rather than set out to confirm them.

You may begin the main part of your research once you have a title expressed in the form of a question. It may be necessary for you to do some background research prior to this, in order to know enough about the topic you have chosen and to be able to formulate the question. However, your main research phase will take place once you have fixed upon your question. There is more information in other chapters on the research process and on essay structure and referencing the work of others. Alternatively, refer to a text focused specifically on writing dissertations. One such text is provided in the Bibliography section towards the end of the book.

4.4: STAGE 4: START A 'RUNNING DOCUMENT' ON THE COMPUTER

- Once you have a question, start a 'running document' on the computer.

- Open a document, consider placing the question on the first page, and then lay out the document as if it were a dissertation.

Include pages such as:

- Abstract/executive summary;

- Contents;

- Introduction;

- Section 1, Section 2, Section 3, Conclusions, Bibliography.

Use this document for notes, questions to yourself, lists of material to research, etc.

Students – and academics – often put off writing. It is difficult to know how to start and one always feels underprepared for the task. Consequently, many begin writing just before a deadline, feel overwhelmed by what they have to do and then become a little panicked. It is relatively easy to overcome some of these problems, although not the lack of motivation to get on with the writing stage, by starting a running document on the computer. Consider setting up a Word document, or similar, split into sections. A dissertation will usually include a title page, an acknowledgements page, an abstract or executive summary page (in which the dissertation is summarised in 100 to 250 words for the marker), a contents page, an introduction, a series of sections or chapters (maybe three or four, however many appear appropriate for the dissertation), conclusions, a bibliography and appendices. Students undertaking socio-legal empirical work (such as interviews or a survey) may include a research methods section or chapter in addition to an introduction, or may include this information in the introduction. Some may also set out a chapter as a literature review, in which academic literature on the subject of the dissertation is discussed, prior to undertaking original empirical research (an analysis of cases, statutes or policy documents, interviews of key people or a survey) on the area. The literature in library-based research tends to be pervasive in the dissertation, rather than contained in a separate chapter. Discuss this with your supervisor if you are unsure about which is most appropriate for your enquiry. Format the titles, add in page numbers, make the document look like a finished document (but without any real content!) and use this as the place to write all your research notes, questions, comments and sources from now on.

4.5: STAGE 5: DISSECT THE QUESTION AND SET OUT YOUR SUB-QUESTIONS

- Analyse your own question.

- List the issues that the question encompasses.

- Divide your main question into its constituent sub-questions.

- Write all of this within the 'running document'.

- Discuss this with your supervisor.

Once you have a robust and relatively static (as opposed to frequently changing) research question, you may want to consider any sub-questions that need to be answered in order to present a final answer to the main question. In a dissertation of around 10,000 words, it is probably only possible to deal with three to five issues effectively, although these too can be narrowed down into sub-sub-questions, if desirable.

The question will contain multiple issues which often need a little thought to dig out and make visible. Each one may form a sub-question. Consider what you need to establish before you can provide an answer to your main question. You may wish to list the sub-questions underneath your main question, by way of identification, as follows:

Dissertation question: To what extent does the UK comply with the European Convention on Human Rights with respect to balancing article 10 (freedom of expression) with article 8 (the right to a private and family life) when questions of privacy versus newspapers' right to publish a story come into conflict?

Sub-question 1: What does the ECHR provide and what does the case law of the ECtHR indicate in relation to the balancing of articles 8 and 10?

Sub-question 2: How does UK legislation address the balancing of privacy and press freedom?

Sub-question 3: How have the press complaints bodies addressed the balancing of privacy and press freedom?

Sub-question 4: How have the UK courts interpreted articles 8 and 10 in the context of privacy cases and freedom of the press?

Conclusion: To what extent does the approach set out in the legislation, and that adopted by press regulation and the courts indicate that the UK complies with the ECHR in relation to the balancing of article 8 and article 10 when questions of privacy versus newspapers' right to publish a story come into conflict?

Naturally there are other ways of interrogating the main question, this is only one way of doing it. But you will see that by thinking about the question in context, it is possible to begin to work out on what you need to focus. There are additional benefits of splitting your main question into its constituent parts beyond helping you with clarity and focus. You should be able to establish whether your question is one that allows you to look at the main issue from a number of different perspectives – if the main question above had been limited to consider only the courts' approach then the dissertation would have been a little thin in content and may not have been so interesting to research. Further, the sub-questions also help with structure. In this example above it would be logical to assign a section or a chapter to each of the sub-questions, and to research each one in turn and discretely as if writing a series of much shorter essays. That tends to be a lot less daunting than tackling the main question as a whole.

Once you have set out the sub-questions it is as well to review the main question and the sub-questions once again to consider whether these appear, if fully answered, to provide a complete answer to the main question. Amend them as necessary. Add these into the running document and move on to the research planning stage.

4.6: STAGE 6: PLAN THE RESEARCH

- Analyse your main question and sub-questions. Do they still make sense to you? Do you need to revise your question, to narrow it or to broaden it?

- List the issues that the sub-questions encompass.

- Make a list of sources that could provide you with material for the dissertation:

You will need to conduct an academic literature review by reading what academics have already concluded on each area (books, journal articles).

- Consider legal sources such as cases, legislation, etc.

- Consider official sources such as consultation papers, governmental reports, Law Commission reports, official statistics, etc.

- Consider whether you wish, and are permitted to, undertake your own empirical research through interviews, questionnaire surveys, observation.

- Note down how each of these types of sources could assist in the dissertation and with what standpoint they may help.

- Plan your research for each of the sub-questions – which one will you tackle first, which sources will you use, how will you go about your research?

- Write all of this within the running document.

- Discuss this with your supervisor.

This is an important stage, because it is probably only now that you can see whether your original question is too broad or too narrow, whether you will have access to the necessary research resources to answer it and indeed whether you even want to engage with the question drafted this way. You will continue to revise your question, and your research, in the light of your deepening knowledge of the area, but now would be a good time to assess, in realistic terms, whether this is the question that you want to take forward. You should do this in conjunction with your supervisor.

Once you have a list of sub-questions, note down what sources of data may provide answers to them, and where those sources can be located. Sources are different types of material that you can use as an evidence base. As lawyers we tend to rely heavily on documentary sources (written texts) that have been generated by others for a range of purposes. We regularly use legislation and case reports, we also refer to the academic literature, meaning books, articles or reports written by academics, or the professional literature written by practitioners or other professional commentators (including professional bodies). Their work will have been informed by earlier literature, legislation and cases, but they may also have referred to studies that used non-legal empirical sources such as interviews, questionnaires or observation to generate data to answer a particular question or they may have generated data themselves using these means. In your study you may decide to confine yourself to legal sources and academic literature sources, or you may wish to look at a broader range of sources (the professional literature, media reports, interest group reports, etc.). You may want to generate your own data by conducting interviews, questionnaire surveys or observation yourself but if you choose to do this you will need to have some training and you will need to gain ethical approval from your university before embarking on it – this can all take time, so do factor this in to your schedule when planning your research and ensure that your supervisor is willing to support you in this approach.

Whatever you decide to do you should use a range of sources for each sub-question, rather than restricting yourself to one source, as the more sources you use, the more likely you are to develop a balanced understanding of the issues and gain multiple forms of evidence with which to assert your arguments. This will provide breadth, depth and authority to your writing. It will help you towards critical analysis, by making links between different aspects of your analysis to reach a higher level of understanding and critique. You will find more information on different sources in Chapter 5.

4.7: STAGE 7: BEGIN RESEARCHING THE INTRODUCTION

- The introduction should explain the state of academic and legal knowledge on the main topic of your dissertation (unless the dissertation contains a separate literature review).

- Conduct a Google Scholar search for academic sources relevant to your topic.

- Consult the library catalogue for sources relevant to your topic.

- Conduct a search of online databases for academic literature and relevant cases and legislation.

- Make notes for these in the running document under the introduction heading.

- Note down the source of the notes (with page numbers), so that these can be turned into footnotes at a later stage.

The introduction in a dissertation is more extensive than an introduction in a traditional coursework essay. The introduction should set out how you have approached your dissertation research, including your research method, unless you have assigned a separate section to explain your method (this is more usual if you are undertaking interviews or a survey yourself). It should explain the nature of the question and the sub-questions and how these aim to provide an answer to the main question. It should refer to academic literature written on the subject of your dissertation, as the background to your study, unless you have assigned a separate chapter as an academic literature review. An academic literature review is simply your analysis of what academics have already concluded on the question – on what they agree and why, on what they disagree and why, how that assists you in answering the question, and then which parts of the question remain unanswered such that you need to undertake primary legal or other research (such as by reading cases for example) so as to answer the question fully. This background provides the platform for your subsequent research on the sub-questions. The introduction should also set out the issues you will consider in the dissertation and explain the structure of the dissertation. In essence it acts as both the background to your study and also as a signpost for what is to follow, including an explanation of your research question and sub-questions.

4.8: STAGE 8: CONDUCT RESEARCH ON EACH SUB-QUESTION

- Follow the steps above for each sub-question.

- It is usual to begin with an academic literature review, setting out which parts of your sub-question have already been satisfactorily answered by academics, and which parts remain unanswered.

- Then consider any relevant primary sources (such as legislation and cases).

- Then consider any other relevant sources such as official reports, policy documents, etc.

- If you are thinking of generating your own data by conducting interviews, a survey or observation, then refer to books on empirical research techniques before embarking on this. Further, ensure you seek approval from your supervisor, and also ethical approval from your university (as needed), particularly if you intend to undertake research involving people (human subjects).

- Make notes in the running document on material for each sub-question.

- Keep in touch with your supervisor.

The next step is to undertake research for each sub-question, as you would approach any other essay. Each sub-question is a mini-essay in itself, with an introduction, a middle section and a conclusion. You will probably need to begin with an academic literature review but there will be additional material that you can draw upon. Consider which sources will be relevant in answer to the question and where they are located. Make notes on each of the sources, preferably in the running document, with full references, including page references, for each source. Discuss your progress with your supervisor before moving on to the next section. Any material that you find while working on one section, which is relevant to another section, can be noted down within the relevant section for use at a later stage. Continue with note-taking until either you have exhausted the cases, legislation, academic works, interviewees or participants, or until you wish to review the notes to date and begin to write them up into paragraphs.

Some students relish the opportunity to break out of the straitjacket of legal sources when they come to undertake a dissertation. This can be a very fruitful pursuit, assuming that you have had previous training in how to use other sources or you are willing to learn how to make use of them and in a context in which your supervisor may have little or no experience of socio-legal techniques so as to be able to guide you. If you are using any data source with which you are not familiar (policy documents, interviews with people such as experts, etc.) then please read up on how to conduct this kind or research before you embark upon it. Make sure too that you have sought ethical approval from the university ethics committee, if you decide to go out into the field and interview people or make use of a survey instrument. Be sure too that you conform to appropriate data collection and storage techniques; just as there are rules about how you select, read, analyse and use cases and legislation so there are rules on how you select, review, analyse and use other forms of data. Interview data is most frequently linked to the disciplines of sociology and psychology; observation to anthropology; surveys to psychology, sociology and marketing; statistics to economics, psychology and sociology; policy documents to policy and political studies. There are some texts set out in the bibliography that may help with the socio-legal research techniques described above and others too. You will need to consider data analysis techniques and not just how to collect the data. You may also wish to read Chapter 5, which addresses how to use evidence (and find evidence) in your writing, as this may provide some assistance with how to locate relevant library-based sources. There is more guidance provided on the companion website too.

4.9: STAGE 9: REVIEW YOUR NOTES FOR EACH SECTION/CHAPTER – WRITE A FIRST DRAFT

- Reread the question.

- Read through the running document and consider whether the sub-questions appear to answer the main question.

- Read the notes you have made for each sub-question.

- Follow the essay writing steps in previous chapters to plan a mini-essay for each sub-question.

- Group issues together that appear similar and keep separate those that appear to be different.

- Construct paragraphs from your notes, using evidence to back up the points being made.

- Reread each section/chapter to review whether it answers the sub-question.

- Consider where there are gaps in your arguments.

- Conduct further research if necessary.

- Repeat the steps until you have fully answered all the sub-questions.

Some people prefer to complete the research phase for a section before starting to write the notes up into paragraphs. Others prefer to do both alongside each other, in order to break up the monotony of note-taking. The writing phase for a dissertation is very similar to the writing phase for an essay, although more extensive. Similar rules apply, however, as set out in Chapter 2. Read through the notes and organise them into themes. Consider how each theme relates to the sub-question. Group any evidence that is relevant to the theme next to that theme and organise themes into a logical order. You are likely to change these around as the dissertation progresses and you will also write and rewrite paragraphs as you go along. However, do not let this prevent you from writing up your notes early on in the dissertation process, as much of the material you write now will be used in one form or another in the final draft. Further, the writing process is part of the way in which we develop our knowledge and it takes time and frequent redrafts to reach a sophisticated answer to each sub-question. It is more satisfying to see the dissertation grow and to edit it down to the word limit later on in the process, rather than to try to construct a dissertation as the deadline approaches.

4.10: Stage 10: Read Through the Sub-questions and Write the Draft Conclusion

- Read through the main question and the sub-questions.

- Read through each dissertation section/chapter.

- Take the conclusion from each section/chapter and copy it into the conclusions section.

- Read your draft conclusions chapter made up of each of the section conclusions.

- Work out your thesis (final answer) and write an overview paragraph or paragraphs so as to set out your final thesis.

- Redraft your conclusion so that your thesis is carried throughout the conclusion, is persuasive, and well communicated.

Each section should contain a conclusion that pulls together a final answer to the sub-questions that you set for that section. The easiest way to approach the dissertation conclusion is to cut and paste each of those conclusions into the final conclusion section, read them through and work out what is your thesis (your final conclusion to the question). It is as well at this stage to have the question in front of you as you read through the conclusions, and to note down your response to the question once you have completed reading the conclusion. You should then redraft your conclusion knowing what is your (tentative) answer to the question. Your final conclusion will also need to explain how each of the sub-questions (and conclusions to those sub-questions) fit together to provide a complete answer to the main question. Conclusions sometimes begin with a discussion of the main question – what the research project has sought to consider – and how the sub-questions seek to do that. You may then wish to write one or two paragraphs in respect of each sub-question, prior to finalising the conclusion with paragraphs providing the final analysis of the main question. Try to avoid introducing new ideas into the conclusion unless they are simply thoughts for the future, as new ideas may detract from your findings and lead the reader to wonder why you did not address them more fully in the main body of your work. You will now need to redraft your dissertation knowing what you have concluded, as the dissertation should read as if you knew the answer before you wrote the first word, rather than as your intellectual journey from confusion at the start to knowledge at the end. There is more detail on this in Chapter 2.

4.11: STAGE 11: FIRST DRAFT POLISHING – OVERVIEW

- Read through the main question and the sub-questions.

- Read through each dissertation section/chapter.

- Check that each section answers the sub-question fully, with evidence to back up any assertions.

- Check that, when read together, the whole dissertation answers the main question, with evidence to back up any assertions.

- If the question is not fully answered, could the question be amended so that the dissertation and the answer do fit?

- If not, then rewrite the dissertation as required.

The first review of your dissertation should focus on whether you have answered your main question and subsequent sub-questions. Take the main question and dissect it, as you would in an exam or for a piece of coursework. Does it really fit with what you have written in your dissertation? If it does not, and if permitted under the module regulations, amend the title so that it does correspond with the task you have undertaken. You will be marked against your question and thus the dissertation must be a full answer to it.

Next, review the sub-questions. Do they appear, when taken together, to answer the main question? Undertake the same steps as discussed for the main question. Then read through each section or chapter to consider whether each one answers the sub-question fully. Each section is similar to a mini-essay and may be as long as a piece of coursework submitted at level 4 (first year undergraduate level). Each should have an introduction, a middle section and a conclusion, in the same way as any other essay. Each section should provide an answer to the sub-question set for that section. And it should read as if you knew the answer when you began writing the introduction, so you will need to redraft each section a few times to ensure that your final level of knowledge of the answer to that sub-question is reflected right from the beginning.

The next step is to read through the introduction. Does the introduction set out how you have approached your dissertation research, including your research method? Does it set out the question and sub-questions? Does it refer to academic literature on the area you have researched? Does it set out the issues you have considered? Does it explain the structure of the dissertation? Does it reflect the understanding you have now having reached your conclusions? Make any changes to your draft, before turning your attention to the conclusion.

Finally, read through the conclusion. Does it pull together each of the conclusions from each of the dissertation sections? Does it provide a final conclusion to the main question, indicating how each of the sub-questions links to provide that answer? You may wish to read through each section conclusion again, before reading the final conclusion, to assist this process.

4.12: STAGE 12: SECOND DRAFT POLISHING – PARAGRAPH MAPPING

- **Read through the dissertation paragraph by paragraph.**
- **Check that the paragraph begins by stating the issue to be discussed within it.**
- **Check that the paragraph contains a discussion of the issue.**

- Check that the paragraph contains authoritative and plentiful evidence to justify the points being made.

- Check that full citations have been included to others' words/ideas and that those citations are included in the bibliography.

- Check that the paragraph is concluded with a sentence or sentences, explaining how the issue relates to the sub-question.

- Check that the paragraphs flow on from one another so that the arguments develop logically, and all similar issues are dealt with together.

- Make any changes.

Read through your draft again, if you can bear it. This time you are mapping each paragraph. Check that each paragraph is clear on the issue being discussed, the evidence in support of the assertions being made and the relevance of the issue to the sub-question. Check too that all sources are fully referenced in footnotes, and that relevant material is contained within the bibliography. Each sub-question should then be related to the main question in the conclusion, to provide a complete answer to the main question. It is also useful to note down on your draft the issue being discussed in each paragraph and then to skim through these notes to ensure there is no repetition. You should also check that similar issues are dealt with together. You may need to move paragraphs around in your draft, maybe even to another section in your dissertation, to cut down on repetition and to assist the development of your arguments. Make any changes and then move on to finishing and polishing your work.

For the brave, and for those aiming at very high marks, a more extensive paragraph redraft may be beneficial. Critical analysis is the key to high marks, as is reducing the amount of description in each paragraph. You may want to reduce your description and increase your analysis by taking your paragraph conclusion to the top of your paragraph, redrafting your middle section so as to be a justification for your analysis, adding a higher level concluding phrase once you have worked through your new conclusion and then repeating the process. This technique is discussed in more detail in Chapter 2. You may be able to collapse multiple paragraphs together in a more dense, but more nuanced piece of analysis; you may even be able to redraft a whole section using this technique and then rewrite your section introduction so as to reflect the new points that you have developed, and the section conclusion similarly. This can be repeated throughout the document. Over time your dissertation should improve considerably.

4.13: STAGE 13: THIRD DRAFT POLISHING – SPELLING, GRAMMAR, PRESENTATION AND FORMATTING

- Check your draft for spelling and grammar mistakes.

- Consider the formatting and presentation requirements set for the dissertation module and make sure your draft conforms to those requirements.

- Make any changes.

This step is best undertaken after you have put your dissertation to one side for a few days. It is always easier to finish and polish a piece of work once you have had some distance from your work (and also some sleep!). Read through your dissertation one final time, to proofread it. Run a spellcheck if you have not done so previously, so as to eliminate as many minor mistakes as possible. Check that sentences flow and that the dissertation is presented in a way that conforms to any formatting and presentation requirements, including line spacing, page numbering and layout. If you have used headings in your dissertation, check them to make sure that all headings of the same level look the same – are they all the same point size, in the same font; are they all bold, or italicised, or underlined? Although you are unlikely to lose a tremendous number of marks for issues such as these, a well-presented dissertation gives an aura of authority and sloppy work does tend to suggest sloppy analysis too. It is as well to project a professional image rather than an unprofessional one. You may wish to refer to Chapter 7 to consider writing style issues. Dissertations should be written in a formal style, unlike this book, which has adopted an informal style. Check, too, that footnotes and endnotes are all typed in a consistent style and that the bibliography is in alphabetical order, that it is complete, groups books with other books, journal articles with other journal articles, websites with other websites, and cases and legislation in separate sections. Make any changes before moving on to the final stage.

4.14: STAGE 14: FINAL CHECK OF ASSESSMENT AND GRADING CRITERIA

- Finally, read through the assessment and grading criteria for the module and check your draft against it.

- Make any changes.

Far more will be expected of a dissertation than a piece of coursework at levels 4 (first year) and 5 (second year). Make sure you have read the assessment and grading criteria before you begin your dissertation, but also read them through again at the end to ensure that your dissertation meets them. Reread any instructions given to you in relation to the dissertation – the number of copies that should be submitted, to whom, and so forth – prior to submitting your work. Then have the courage to hand it in, and congratulate yourself on having finished an extensive piece of writing.

Next steps:

1 Check your progress on the flow chart to see where you are in the dissertation process.

2 Review what you have done so far and consider which steps you have completed but which, on reflection, you may need to revisit.

3 Plan out your time between now and the deadline. Do you need to change anything about your work pattern in order to ensure successful completion?

4 Consider whether you need to see your supervisor to discuss progress. Have you got any written work ready to send to him or her in advance so that your meeting may be a productive one?

If you are in any doubt about research or referencing, you may wish to read the next two chapters.

SUMMARY

The following approach may assist in researching, structuring and writing a dissertation, although you should discuss your approach with your supervisor.

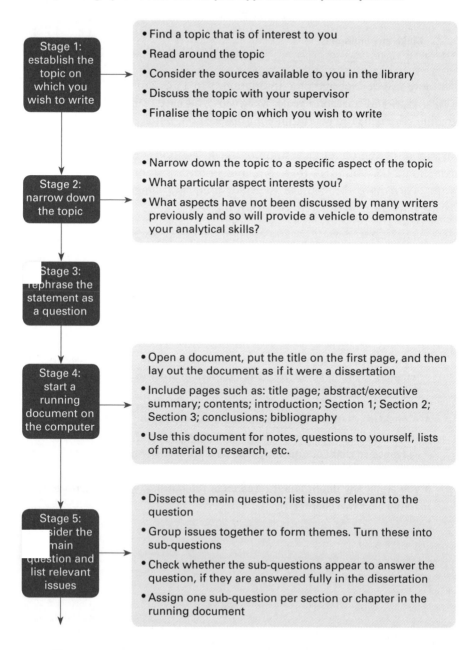

Stage 1: establish the topic on which you wish to write

- Find a topic that is of interest to you
- Read around the topic
- Consider the sources available to you in the library
- Discuss the topic with your supervisor
- Finalise the topic on which you wish to write

Stage 2: narrow down the topic

- Narrow down the topic to a specific aspect of the topic
- What particular aspect interests you?
- What aspects have not been discussed by many writers previously and so will provide a vehicle to demonstrate your analytical skills?

Stage 3: rephrase the statement as a question

Stage 4: start a running document on the computer

- Open a document, put the title on the first page, and then lay out the document as if it were a dissertation
- Include pages such as: title page; abstract/executive summary; contents; introduction; Section 1; Section 2; Section 3; conclusions; bibliography
- Use this document for notes, questions to yourself, lists of material to research, etc.

Stage 5: consider the main question and list relevant issues

- Dissect the main question; list issues relevant to the question
- Group issues together to form themes. Turn these into sub-questions
- Check whether the sub-questions appear to answer the question, if they are answered fully in the dissertation
- Assign one sub-question per section or chapter in the running document

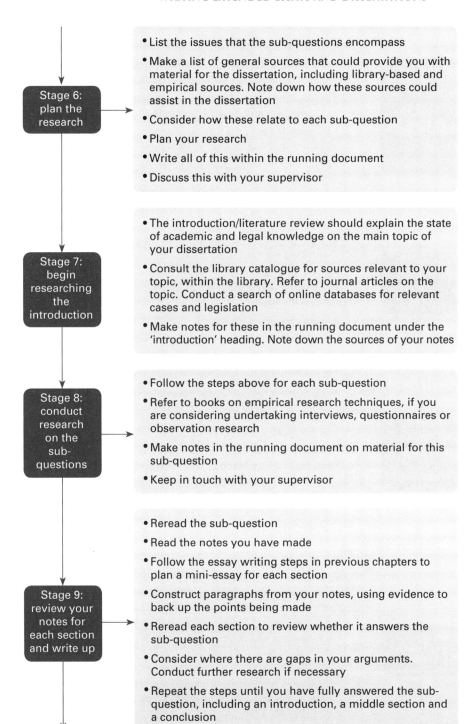

Stage 6: plan the research

- List the issues that the sub-questions encompass
- Make a list of general sources that could provide you with material for the dissertation, including library-based and empirical sources. Note down how these sources could assist in the dissertation
- Consider how these relate to each sub-question
- Plan your research
- Write all of this within the running document
- Discuss this with your supervisor

Stage 7: begin researching the introduction

- The introduction/literature review should explain the state of academic and legal knowledge on the main topic of your dissertation
- Consult the library catalogue for sources relevant to your topic, within the library. Refer to journal articles on the topic. Conduct a search of online databases for relevant cases and legislation
- Make notes for these in the running document under the 'introduction' heading. Note down the sources of your notes

Stage 8: conduct research on the sub-questions

- Follow the steps above for each sub-question
- Refer to books on empirical research techniques, if you are considering undertaking interviews, questionnaires or observation research
- Make notes in the running document on material for this sub-question
- Keep in touch with your supervisor

Stage 9: review your notes for each section and write up

- Reread the sub-question
- Read the notes you have made
- Follow the essay writing steps in previous chapters to plan a mini-essay for each section
- Construct paragraphs from your notes, using evidence to back up the points being made
- Reread each section to review whether it answers the sub-question
- Consider where there are gaps in your arguments. Conduct further research if necessary
- Repeat the steps until you have fully answered the sub-question, including an introduction, a middle section and a conclusion

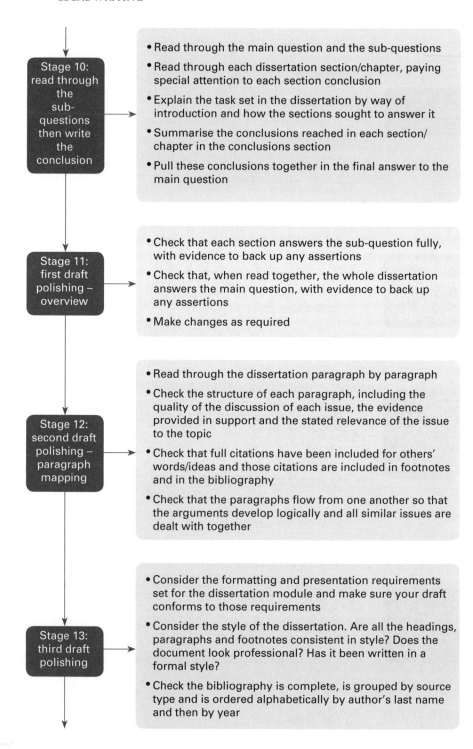

Stage 10: read through the sub-questions then write the conclusion

- Read through the main question and the sub-questions
- Read through each dissertation section/chapter, paying special attention to each section conclusion
- Explain the task set in the dissertation by way of introduction and how the sections sought to answer it
- Summarise the conclusions reached in each section/chapter in the conclusions section
- Pull these conclusions together in the final answer to the main question

Stage 11: first draft polishing – overview

- Check that each section answers the sub-question fully, with evidence to back up any assertions
- Check that, when read together, the whole dissertation answers the main question, with evidence to back up any assertions
- Make changes as required

Stage 12: second draft polishing – paragraph mapping

- Read through the dissertation paragraph by paragraph
- Check the structure of each paragraph, including the quality of the discussion of each issue, the evidence provided in support and the stated relevance of the issue to the topic
- Check that full citations have been included for others' words/ideas and those citations are included in footnotes and in the bibliography
- Check that the paragraphs flow from one another so that the arguments develop logically and all similar issues are dealt with together

Stage 13: third draft polishing

- Consider the formatting and presentation requirements set for the dissertation module and make sure your draft conforms to those requirements
- Consider the style of the dissertation. Are all the headings, paragraphs and footnotes consistent in style? Does the document look professional? Has it been written in a formal style?
- Check the bibliography is complete, is grouped by source type and is ordered alphabetically by author's last name and then by year

Stage 14: final check of assessment and grading criteria and submission

- Read through the assessment and grading criteria for the module and check your draft against it
- Make any last-minute changes
- Hand it in!

5

HOW TO APPLY RESEARCH FINDINGS IN YOUR WRITING

You will need to research relevant law and related issues in order to answer your essay or problem question answer.[1] Research can be daunting, as there is a lot of information available and it is difficult to know how to find relevant information. You should be able to navigate your way through the research process successfully if you break it down into manageable steps. The key stages in good library-based research for essays and problem questions are as follows:

5.1: KEY STAGES IN THE RESEARCH PROCESS

- **Identify your question and dissect it.**

- **Carry out background research if necessary, to ensure that you understand the question. This should usually include reading through any lecture and tutorial notes on the topics covered by the question.**

- **Carry out textbook reading on the topic, making notes relevant to the question.**

- **Carry out research using the library catalogue to find any other academic texts relevant to the question. You will need to develop keywords so as to do these searches. Make any additional notes that are relevant.**

- **Research cases and legislation that are relevant to the question and read important ones in full. Cases will be accessible via the online databases (Lexis and Westlaw) and legislation via the legislation.gov. uk website as well as the databases above. Important cases and**

---

1 Unless of course you are in an exam, in which case you will have done this before you enter the exam room, through revising the law and academic opinion on the law and legal concepts that you are likely to address in your exam answers.

legislation will often be highlighted in your textbook. It is good practice to read these in full and in the original (rather than in the textbook). This is particularly important for problem questions.

● Research academic opinion on the topic by reading journal articles or academic texts or official reports and policy documents and make notes on any issues raised that are relevant to the question. This is particularly useful for assessments, such as essays, that go beyond asking questions about the application of law to facts. You will access these via Google Scholar and databases such as Lexis, Westlaw and Hein Online (via your e-library).

● Read through all your notes and make a list of key issues from your notes, which are relevant to answering the question.

● Highlight any evidence you have in your notes in support of or against the key issues you will discuss in your essay.

● Make sure that you keep a record of all the sources you have used, including the page references of the material you have noted down.

● Plan your essay.

● Begin writing your essay.

You should spend a considerable period of time considering what the question is asking you to write about. This is the diagnostic phase of your role, and your ability to do well in the assessment is dependent on correctly diagnosing the legal or socio-legal issues that you are being asked to discuss.

5.2: How to Start Your Research: What is Your Question?

● If you have been given a question, dissect this first and make sure that you are clear on what it is asking you to write about. This will make it easier to be focused during your research phase.

● If you have to set your own question for a dissertation, then define your research area in broad terms but make sure you have translated your research into a question rather than a statement to begin with.

As indicated earlier in the Introduction and Chapters 2 (essays) and 3 (problem questions), understanding the question is the key to success. Either rewrite the question in different terms to be sure that you have understood it, or list the main issue that is the subject of the question and then any sub-issues that you should consider in the light of the main question. If you have not been given a question, then you need to define one for yourself. There is some guidance on this in the previous chapter. You should be able to develop some basic keywords (related to the question) having dissected the question and worked out the sub-questions – these will be used to conduct later stages of your research. But first begin with the material that you have to hand already.

5.3: USE YOUR EXISTING NOTES

- Pull out your lecture notes and any other notes you have on the main subject of the question and read those through. This is your background research. Look back at the question.

- Write down any things from your notes that are relevant to the question, including any evidence you have that backs up the points you have noted down.

You will hopefully now have a piece of paper or a document on screen that has the question written out at the top with a few lines underneath, which set out what the question is asking you to do. You may have organised your document into sections, one for each main aspect of the question, or for each sub-question too. It is now time to turn to your lecture and tutorial notes to consider what material may be relevant to the question. This stage of your research will be made considerably easier if you have a completed set of good quality notes. You will be taught for the most part of your degree programme through lectures and tutorials, sometimes referred to as seminars. You need to make the most of the limited contact time you have with academic staff, as this will reduce the amount of extra reading you need to do yourself in order to understand the basics of each topic. The lecture should take you through the key issues of a topic and, if you have made useful notes, these will form the basis of your background research.

5.3.1 NOTE-TAKING IN LECTURES AND TUTORIALS

Lecturers usually make a point, then expand upon the point and then provide evidence to back it up and further explanation to illustrate it. You do not need to write all of this down and the chances are that you will not be able to keep up, even if you do try to take down notes verbatim. It is better to listen to what the lecturer is saying, to write down the point that is being discussed and take a note of any evidence that is provided to back up the point (usually this will be a case, a piece of legislation or a theorist's viewpoint), rather than all the detail. This is not easy, and will take practice, but a transcript of the lecture will not make that much sense either. In addition, it may be useful to develop a way of abbreviating words that keep cropping up in the topic so as to speed up your note-taking. You will need to be consistent, otherwise it may be difficult to decipher later on; you may want to write out the word or phrase in full then add your abbreviation in brackets just after it, then use the abbreviation from then on in the lecture. You may also wish to come up with your own standard abbreviations for frequently used words and phrases for all your note-taking (for example, I use *incl* for included or include, *w/* for without, *b/* for because, etc. in all my notes) and/or take those that are often used (*e.g.* for 'for example', *re* for 'in relation to' or 'as regards', *pro* for 'in favour of' or 'a strength', *con* for 'against' or 'a weakness'). One example of note-taking (linear note-taking) in lectures would be as follows:

Parliamentary supremacy lecture

Meaning: Parliament (P.) has supreme legislative power: it can make, amend or repeal any law.

Main theorist Dicey, Jennings modified Dicey's theory, there are other views too, see e.g. Wade. The Theory is not set out in law, but has developed through theory instead, so is parliamentary supremacy (PS) political or legal?

3 parts to theory:
A. P. can make, change, repeal any law without any restrictions.
B. The courts cannot question the legal validity of an Act of P. nor can anyone else.
C. To ensure that P. remains supreme, an earlier P. cannot bind a later one.

Evidence:
A. *Burmah Oil v. Lord Advocate* [1965] AC 75, War Damage Act 1965
See e.g. Jennings in *The Law of the Constitution* smoking on the streets of Paris.

B. Traditional interpretation: *British Railways Board v. Pickin* [1974] AC 765

Lord Reid quote at 782

But see alternative view (cf): Lord Woolf in 'Droit Public – English Style' [1995] Public Law 57, says there may even be limits on P. if it enacts legislation that is extreme and in total breach of human rights.

C. Dicey's traditional view as above. But, redefinition theory – Jennings, Heuston, Wade. See Parliament Acts 1911 & 1949 re discussion on manner and form.
ECA 1972 – has Parliament bound future P. through membership of EU?
EU Act 2011 – referendum now required before any more UK powers ceded to the EU.

Note art 34 of the Lisbon Treaty, exit clause from the EU so Lord Justice Laws' approach in *Thoburn* re PS being retained, but EU law supreme while P. so allows by keeping ECA 1972 in force.

...

This extract demonstrates the way in which many lectures operate. The lecturer will often begin by providing a brief overview of the topic so that you have a cursory understanding before you get into the detail. Often the main themes are spelt out at this stage, and it helps to note these down, preferably leaving yourself some space so that you can go back and fill in detail and evidence under each heading when you read the relevant textbook chapter. If you cannot do that you may wish to number or notate each of the themes so that you can match up the detail and evidence with the theme at a later stage in subsequent notes you make from your reading. It may help you to organise your notes and could also save you time in the lecture and afterwards. The lecturer will often move on to take each of the themes in turn, and provide a more detailed explanation plus evidence to illustrate the points being made. This evidence is often extensive. There may be case and statutory citations and quotes from scholars and practitioners. You may not be able to get all of this down, but as long as you have the citations you can look them up later if you need to. You may have access to the lecturer's PowerPoint slides or similar upon which the citations and main points appear. Indeed, you may be provided with a copy of the PowerPoint slides in advance and if so, and if you make notes on a laptop or tablet, then you may want to make your notes directly onto the PowerPoint pages by using the handout function or notes function in the PowerPoint program.

There are as many ways of taking notes as there are people, and your views on useful notes may change over time. Some people prefer to draw spider diagrams or flow charts, for example; others to divide their paper into sections and allocate different sections to different types of information, that is, one column for headings, another for summaries of key points, another for related evidence, and so forth (Cornell notes: see below).

Lecture (or other) Notes: Heading	
Key points	**Detail on each of the key points**
(similar to the headings in the linear notes example above)	**(similar to the detail in the A, B and C sections in the linear notes above)**
Summary (done just after the lecture, after reading through the notes above so that you can consolidate your knowledge)	

With practice you will find a method that works for you.

 Do refer to the companion website at www.routledge.com/cw/ webley for examples of different forms of note-taking, if you would like to consider which type is likely to prove most useful for you. These will help for all forms of note-taking and not just those for lecture notes.

Most lecturers will use visual aids or handouts to highlight the important issues, or will repeat the issues so that you can take them down. You will be able to supplement these notes with notes from textbook reading, so do not panic if you think that you have missed a point. You can check with the lecturer at the end of the lecture as well, if needs be. You will not be tested on whether you can remember everything that has been said in the lecture, but you will be tested on whether you understand the topic. Try not to miss lectures, as someone else's notes will not be written in the same way as your own and will be no substitute for missing the lecture. Finally, do not ask your lecturer for his or her notes. You will not make yourself popular by admitting that you have missed the lecture and the chances are that the lecturer will not have a set of notes that make any sense to you anyway. Many of us talk from bullet points or the PowerPoint presentation we are using, rather than having a set of written notes in front of us.

Now that you are familiar with the key principles, you may wish to look back at your original keywords list that you developed after dissecting the question, and add additional refinement (extra words) so as to make your research more focused.

5.3.2 INTEGRATING LECTURE AND TUTORIAL NOTES WITH TEXTBOOK NOTES

You will need to bring together multiple sources of notes – lecture notes, notes from your reading, including the textbook, cases, statutes and journal articles, and your answers to tutorial questions, too. One of the difficulties is that students often do not have particularly effective notes from their tutorial preparation and this hampers their ability to pull their lecture and tutorial notes together. It is a long-standing sport among students to see who can 'wing' the tutorial the most effectively. Of course, you may find that you can get through a tutorial or seminar unprepared, but it will be of very little use to you in the long run, sadly, because the preparation is actually the key to success.

Tutorials and seminars are designed to test your knowledge to date and to make sure that you understand the tutorial topic. The questions that have been set are the vehicle for your tutor to examine your understanding and application and to deal with areas of misunderstanding or confusion. They are not designed for a tutor to give you an answer that you can learn for the exam. In fact, if they were, then you would most likely do very badly indeed in the exams, unless you were asked exactly the same question again. As I hope this book illustrates, legal writing is about demonstrating your understanding and application, not your memory. Consequently good preparation for tutorials and seminars allows you to test your understanding and to practise your question dissection technique and essay and problem question planning skills, even if you do not write full answers to all the questions that have been set. You may be asked to hand in a written answer to the question, but even if this is not the practice in your law school, it is as well to write an answer, even if only in note form, so that you get used to working out what questions are asking. Writing an essay or problem question plan, with evidence under each issue, will make it easier for you to participate in the class and also for your tutor to check whether you understand the topic fully. It will also develop your diagnostic technique. And your notes will be of much more use to you when the assessments come around too.

Many first-year undergraduates discover too late that they have lots of sets of notes and none of them match up very easily. Some decide to remedy this by adopting one approach to all their notes, or to use one system for lecture/tutorial and textbook notes and another for primary sources, or for particular types of activity (for example preparations for assessed and non-assessed written work versus notes to use towards exam preparation). Many new law students ask how best to integrate their lecture and tutorial notes with textbook notes that they take so as to augment their knowledge of a topic. They indicate that they are drowning in lots of sets of notes on a similar topic. One way to cope with this is to make your notes from separate sources in separate documents and then pull them together into one overview document, which will act as a revision aid as well as a consolidation aid. Or you may wish to allow space in your lecture notes for any textbook or primary source notes that you make later on the topic. Some people start a new page for each new main heading or idea raised by the lecturer (or new PowerPoint slide), giving them room to add in notes that they make when they read the case, legislation, article, etc. that was mentioned in relation to that heading or idea. That way you will have all your notes in one place, which will make preparation easier for tutorials and also for assessments.

Parliamentary supremacy lecture

Meaning: Parliament (P.) has supreme legislative power: it can make, amend or repeal any law.

Main theorist Dicey, Jennings modified Dicey's theory, there are other views too, see e.g. Wade. The Theory is not set out in law, but has developed through theory instead, so is parliamentary supremacy (PS) political or legal?

[Add in here from your reading a brief summary on Dicey's theory, Jennings' modifications to Dicey's theory, and any other theorists who occur in your reading. You are likely to only need to add a couple of sentences per theorist but reference your source and the page number (you may need this for anything you later write; see Chapter 6) in case you do need more detail at a later stage]

3 parts to theory:
A. P. can make, change, repeal any law without any restrictions.

B. The courts cannot question the legal validity of an Act of P. nor can anyone else.

C. To ensure that P. remains supreme, an earlier P. cannot bind a later one.

Evidence:

A. *Burmah Oil v. Lord Advocate* [1965] AC 75, War Damage Act 1965

[Leave a space here so that when you read **Burmah Oil** you can add in a summary of the ratio, and any quotes from the judgments that are evidence for the PS point. Again, be sure to add a full reference including page or paragraph numbers, so that you can check back and/or use the material in written work]

[Continue to add in material from the textbook, for explanation, and from the primary sources by way of evidence, for the rest of the lecture]

If using the Cornell notes system you would need to leave space in your notes for additional key points and then the detail associated with those key points. You may also amend your summary at the bottom of the page, once you have completed your notes and reread them. Other students annotate their lecture notes with figures or other symbols, so as to allow two sets of notes to be matched up; for example the symbol # may indicate those passages in the lecture and other notes that relate to parliamentary supremacy as a political theory, and those marked with † may indicate those passages that relate to parliamentary supremacy as a legal theory. Others, instead, make all their notes in electronic form, embedding links between the electronic documents so that they can click through from one to the other, and they host them in the cloud so that they can access them from anywhere (similar in style to the e-book version of this text, which allows you to click through to the companion website).

Alternatively, you may wish to incorporate your lecture notes into your textbook notes. To do this you would need to read through your lecture notes before you begin to read the textbook, then copy across or summarise the relevant parts of your lecture material alongside the matching material from the textbook. This is quite fiddly to do to begin with, but it does mean that you have one set of notes to use as the basis for your tutorial preparation. It may also help at the revision stage. Your approach may depend on whether you take notes electronically or on paper, or on whether you prefer diagrammatic or text-based approaches to note-taking. You may want to have a look at the note-taking examples on the companion website and then experiment to find out which work best for you. There is guidance later on in this chapter on making notes from textbooks and other sources. The next step is to plan your research by working out what else you need to know or need to consider further.

5.4: PLAN YOUR RESEARCH

- Plan your research.

- What sub-questions do you have? Where will you find the answers?

- Consider academic sources (books and journal articles), legal sources (legislation and cases), official and policy sources (consultation papers and policy documents).

- Consider how you will access them – in the library via the library catalogue, in the e-library through the databases, through the internet using Google Scholar, from government or the parliament's website.

- With which aspects of the question will each of these sources be likely to help you?

A good essay will contain information from a range of authoritative sources including academic sources such as books and journal articles, legal sources such as cases and legislation, and sometimes from official documents such as consultation papers, policy documents or research reports. You may also include your own fieldwork if you have done a questionnaire survey or you have interviewed people as well. Most undergraduate research for coursework will be library-based, although extended essays and dissertations do lend themselves to non-documentary empirical research as well as library-based research.

It is hard to know where to look for information in a large physical and electronic library at first, particularly if you are not used to doing research. Consider the range of sources available in the library and what these could contribute to your essay or problem question answer. Write a list of sources and how these kinds of sources may help you with your essay question. Refer to any library guides available for your library to help you to become increasingly proficient at finding relevant sources quickly and effectively. The library (including the e-library) is one of the key tools that we use as lawyers, as is our knowledge of how to select, read and draw out information from authoritative sources and then apply that knowledge in context. Just as doctors understand how to make use of the prescription drugs that they have at their disposal, we have to understand the range of sources we have and how to deploy them. Given that most undergraduate and GDL work will relate to the law as written (cases, legislation, commentary on those sources) it is important that you become expert in using your library including your e-library, and planning your research by considering the types of relevant sources and how they may help, can assist with this.

5.5: LEGAL RESEARCH: KEY WORDS

- What do you need to know? What is your question/are your questions?

- Do you understand the sub-question or sub-issues you have been asked to consider? If not, where will you look for information on these?

- Which keywords will you use to search for relevant resources stored electronically?

Your lecture and textbook notes are a good place to start your research, but they should not be the only sources that you refer to – they are the foundations for what is to come next, but they cannot be where you stop. You also need to read the important cases in their full reported form (rather than in the textbook) and to read any relevant legislation in its original form as well. You may need to refer to official reports or policy documents or statistics to answer some types of question. Journal articles are a good source of information on current academic debates on the law and legal theory, and government reports may provide evidence of proposals for legal reform. You need to refer to a variety of sources to give depth to your understanding and to your written work.

One of the major issues we all face is how to narrow down our electronic searches so as to find targeted sources rather than so many that we cannot possibly get through them all. It may be necessary to use very targeted keywords so as to focus your searches. For example, if your question is about parliamentary supremacy and you put those words into Google Scholar you will find around 104,000 results. Some of those results will relate to the UK, but others to Australia, New Zealand, etc., which all operate systems of parliamentary supremacy. So, unless your question asks you something that requires a comparative approach, you will need to add 'UK' or England and Wales, Scotland or Northern Ireland into your keyword search. This would narrow the hit list to a third of its original size.

But your keywords will likely need to be refined further. Look back at your question and consider what it is that you are being asked to focus on (for example, is parliamentary supremacy a political or a legal principle) and then add in that detail to the keyword search too. Your keywords will expand, and in contrast the number of hits will contract, for example:

> Our original question:
> *'The British Parliament was once supreme.' Discuss with reference to Britain's membership of the EU and its obligations in relation to the European Convention on Human Rights (ECHR).*

> *Which we dissected to establish that the focus was:*
>
> *To examine the traditional theory and the redefinition theory (and any others we come across in our research) of parliamentary supremacy and consider the extent to which those different approaches to the theory reflect the constitutional position given the UK's membership of the EU and Council of Europe.*

Our keywords therefore need to include:

- parliamentary supremacy theory [$c.$110,000 hits on Google Scholar]; but "parliamentary supremacy" theory [$c.$6,330 hits]; and
- UK [reduced to $c.$5,400 when UK is added to the keywords above]; or "United Kingdom" [reduced to $c.$3,450]; and
- EU [reduced to $c.$2, 870]; or "European Union" [reduced to $c.$2,320]; or membership of "European Union" [reduced to $c.$563]; and
- "Council of Europe" [reduced to $c.$151].

So by generating 12 keywords from the question and adding them all in to the search engine, with appropriate " " to join words together as phrases, we have managed to filter over 110,000 to 151.

You may also want to use some of the more sophisticated keyword techniques associated with different types of database. You will need to check how they operate for each one (each database has a help section to show you the particular features). Some search engines and databases allow you to enclose phrases in quotation marks so that the search looks for documents that contain those phrases rather than those in which the individual words appear. Others allow you to add phrases such as 'AND' to connect words, or others to search for alternatives or to exclude certain things too. You will find links to further sources of help with this on the companion website.

5.6: WHERE TO LOOK FOR THE ANSWERS TO YOUR RESEARCH QUESTIONS

- **Actual law:** legislation and cases.

- **Legal opinion/arguments/theories:** books and journal articles and possibly some academic blogs (see for example the UK Constitutional Law Group blog).

- **Public opinion:** newspapers, polls.

- **Research findings by academics:** books and journal articles as well as research reports.

- **Government policy:** official reports and consultation documents.

A good piece of written work refers to a variety of sources in order to prove the points that are being made in each paragraph. Some points will be backed up with reference to case law or legislation, some with references to legal opinion in books or law journals. It is essential that you use 'authority' or 'authoritative evidence' so that you can persuade the reader that your points are well considered and sustainable. You will need to look through the library catalogue to find books that are relevant to your research. The e-library catalogue will also provide details of the journals that are held in the library. The key is to make sure that the books you use are current, not out of date, as law books tend to be updated frequently as the law changes.

You will also likely need to refer to case law too, particularly for problem question answers. Cases can be found in the law report bound volumes in the library or via one of the electronic facilities such as All England Direct, Lexis-Nexis, Westlaw and Lawtel. Legislation can be found in *Halsbury's Statutes* and *Halsbury's Statutory Instruments* in print form or via Lexis. Commentary on the law (similar to an encyclopaedia on the law) is available via *Halsbury's Laws Direct* in electronic form via Lexis too. Some of the electronic facilities also have recent legislation contained within their databases, but you can always access newer legislation online (www.legislation.gov.uk) as well as some older legislation from the Office of Public Sector Information (www.opsi.gov.uk/psi). Bills and their progress can be found via the Parliament website, which contains a wealth of other material too (www.parliament.uk). European legislation can be found in the *Official Journal L Series*, which is available in print form or in electronic form via the Europa website (http://europa.eu). You may also make use of EUR-Lex, which is a free online European Law service (http://eur-lex.europa.eu/en/index.htm).

Your law school is likely to run training in how to use the law library and the electronic sources, and it is as well to get to grips with your research tools as soon as you can, and preferably before you need to use them for your coursework. Ask at the library counter if you are in any doubt, as they will be able to point you in the right direction, refer you to research guides or tell you when training takes place. More detailed information on legal research is provided in books by other authors, references for some of which are given towards the end of the book.

Many students are very adept at using the internet as a research tool. This is a great skill and can prove extremely useful, as long as you locate authoritative sources. Search engines such as Google Scholar can help enormously with that, along with non-internet-based electronic databases as mentioned previously. Most law essays and the vast majority of problem question answers should rely heavily on the research evidence from authoritative sources such as judicial comment in cases, the text of legislation, academic opinion from textbooks and from journal articles. Essays may draw upon these sources, and others besides, such as official reports, may provide evidence of government policy or other state agencies. That is not to say that you cannot provide evidence from other sources, but it is important to consider what these sources tell you. Newspaper reports are evidence of what has come to the public's attention or of public opinion itself. They are not legal authority and they should not be used to support comments of what has happened in a particular case (unless they are from the Law Reports section), nor are they necessarily evidence of facts, as we know that newspapers can get things wrong. Internet pages are also potentially difficult to use as evidence for certain propositions you may be making. The content of an internet page is only as authoritative as the author. Anyone with some computer skills can post information on the internet. It does not mean that the information is accurate, so do not rely on anything unless you are sure that the source is a good one and is very likely to be accurate. Your analysis will be judged on the basis of your evidence, and if your evidence is of poor quality then your mark will reflect this.

Equally, some internet sites are funded by groups with very particular political agendas. The content of their sites will reflect their political views. This does not mean that the information cannot be used in written work, but it is important to understand the authors' standpoint and to explain that the material may be partial. It may only put forward evidence in favour of their views, while leaving out evidence that is equally valid but against their views. The standpoint of any author tells the reader about how s/he will have used evidence in the document. Your arguments will have added weight if you are able to explain the author's standpoint and subject the author's arguments to analysis yourself.

You will make use of primary and secondary sources in your research. Primary sources are extremely important and should form a major part of your research. These are sources that give you the most authoritative evidence. A primary source is 'the thing' itself, and not someone's interpretation of 'the thing'. Secondary sources (there are tertiary, etc., too) are sources through which others give their opinion or their interpretation of something. The boxes that follow provide an illustration of primary and secondary sources.

Primary sources of law: Legislation

The legislation in Halsbury's Statutes or the official government site for legislation www.legislation.gov.uk, or in one of the scholarly legal databases (Westlaw, LexisNexis, Lawtel)

Things to check:

- Is the legislation in force?
- Is the copy of the legislation that you have up to date?
- Is the legislation applicable to this jurisdiction (Scotland only, Wales only, Northern Ireland only, England only, a combination of all four)?
- Is there associated primary or secondary legislation that you need to read too?
- Is the legislation in the process of reform?

Primary sources of law: Cases

The official application of the law – cases reported in the Law Reports (copies of which may be found in scholarly legal databases Westlaw, LexisNexis, Lawtel)

Things to check:

- Does the case squarely relate to this issue that you are considering?
- What is its precedent value – the seniority of the court? Binding or persuasive?
- Is the precedent still subsisting?
- Are there other cases that affirm this legal interpretation?
- Are there cases that contradict this legal interpretation? If so, how? What difference would it make?
- If the case is applied to the facts in the problem in front of you, what would be the result and why?

You may also make use of secondary sources. Secondary sources in this context would include:

Secondary sources for the law

- **Commentary on the law** – *Halsbury's Laws of England* – in the reference section of the library or available via Lexis. General or specific comment or analysis by academics and practitioners, which are published in academic journal articles, academic books, textbooks. Many journal articles can be found on the scholarly legal databases. Books etc., via the library catalogue.

- **Less authoritative commentary** – wider public interpretation of the law (may be authoritative, may be totally inaccurate). This commentary may be found in many fora.

You will be asked to undertake research on areas other than the strict law, or government policy. For each of these you need to consider what question you are asking, in order to identify what would be a primary source of information on that, and what would be a comment/interpretation and thus a secondary source. You will need to use multiple sources of research evidence in your essay or problem question answer. Just as in natural science (when a scientist performs an experiment at least three times to judge the validity of the initial finding), a good researcher will seek multiple sources of evidence before reaching a conclusion. One source is not enough to make a proper assessment of a situation; it will also be insufficient to demonstrate the breadth and depth of your research skills and your scholarly credentials. One case is not evidence of the law, nor is one textbook or one journal article evidence of academic opinion as it may be only evidence of one person's academic opinion. Do not finish your research just because you have found one source to evidence each point. You must conduct broad and deep research before you finalise your own conclusions.

Another issue, which is particularly relevant in relation to sources found on the internet, is how authoritative is the source that you are considering? Your point is only ever as good as the evidence that you provide in support of it. But how do you know if your evidence is any good? How do you judge the authority of the source that you are reading? You should ask yourself the following questions:

How to judge the authority of a source

- **Who is commenting?**

- **What is their standing and expertise?**

● **Are they commenting on something within their expertise?**

● **Have others reviewed this person's view and endorsed it (in other words, has the work been reviewed by an editor or by other academic/ practitioner reviewers)?**

Books and journal articles are much easier to rely upon, as they have been through some form of review process to ensure that at least basic standards of accuracy are met. However, some material on the internet will not have been reviewed or edited. Indeed, some of it will be misleading or possibly incorrect. Many lecturers will consider open-access sources that can be freely edited by anyone, such as Wikipedia, as unreliable in view of this fact. Some entries will be written to a very high standard and others will not. On that basis it is probably safer not to rely on them, but to find a more readily authoritative source that you can use instead.

Finally, textbooks are a good source of information, but a piece of coursework should contain a range of sources, not just references to the set textbook. Revision aids are just that – revision aids. They are good sources of basic information but they are not sufficiently authoritative to be a major source of evidence for a piece of coursework. Try to broaden out your research to include a range of sources, authors from a range of standpoints, and to use authoritative sources.

Before we move on to the next issue, it may perhaps help were we to consider the research steps required to locate authoritative evidence for the essay question set out in Chapter 2 or a problem question as set out in Chapter 3. After dissecting the question and reading through all lecture and tutorial notes, a relatively standard approach to research would be as follows:

1. Library catalogue search to find further textbooks (other than the one(s) used for the tutorial topic related to the question). You may also locate more scholarly texts (non-textbooks) written for an academic audience. These may be more difficult to understand but would provide good research evidence. These should be authoritative secondary sources.

2. A LexisNexis and/or Westlaw search for relevant cases, legislation, journal articles. This type of research will give you primary (cases and legislation) and secondary authoritative sources (journal articles).

3. A visit to the EU's website (http://europa.eu) and the Council of Europe's website (http://hub.coe.int/) may provide some background to help you with your study, or you may wish to use the search facilities to find primary and secondary sources there too. These would also be authoritative.

4   A Google Scholar search may provide you with more journal articles, which may assist you in writing your essay and providing evidence in support of your points. It may also provide you with academic research reports. Most of the sources here will be secondary and authoritative. It is well worth being logged in to your university account when you do a Google Scholar search, as were you to want to access a journal article via Google Scholar and were your university to subscribe to the e-journal, then you would be able to use the link on the right-hand side of the screen that would take you straight through to the e-journal via your e-library. Were you not logged in then you may find that you could only access the journal abstract (summary) and would be asked to pay for the full version.

5   If you do wish to do a traditional internet search, using Google or one of the other search engines, be aware that many of the sources will lack authority and it may be difficult to authenticate the contents of many of the sites.

Now that we have considered, in brief, how to undertake research, we shall turn to how to make use of research findings in written work.

5.7: WHAT NEXT?

- Make notes on the issues that you need to answer in the question from your sources.

- Do not make general notes on the topic as you will not use that information and your effort will be wasted.

- Note down the full citations as you will need to reference your work.

Once you have found sources of information that are relevant to your essay or problem question, you need to begin making notes on the sources. Photocopying or scanning the material and highlighting passages in the text is not the same as making notes! You may find it useful to highlight sections, but then you need to translate those sections into something that you can use. Your notes need to state the point that the highlighted section proves or disproves, as a quote is only evidence for the point you are making; it is not a point in itself. Return to your question frequently to refresh your memory about the task you have been set, and make notes according to the question rather than according to the topic. Ask yourself whether you will use the material you are writing down, and if not then do not take the time and energy to make notes on it.

5.8: HOW DO I MAKE NOTES FROM MY READING?

- Do not make notes straightaway; read a paragraph or short section through first. Consider using one of the speed-reading techniques, if you are reading with a purpose (such as to answer a question).

- If reading so as to understand a topic (textbook reading, for example), identify what point each paragraph is making. Make a note of that point; try to avoid writing out the paragraph again in your own words! Make a note of any evidence the author uses to back up the point.

- Only quote the text you are reading if it is essential that the exact words used are read by the marker or reader (you may need the exact words of the statute or of the judge). Try to summarise the point in your own words in one or two sentences as frequently as possible.

- Repeat for each short section.

- Always keep a full citation of or reference to your source, including an accurate page reference. You will need a statutory/legislative reference and section number (or equivalent) for legislation and you may need a paragraph number for material from some cases as well as the full case citation and the judge who gave the judgment that you are citing.

Given that as lawyers we spend so much time reading, we also spend a lot of time note-taking. It may take some time before you become proficient at reading large quantities of material and extracting the essential information and reducing it to note form. You can maximise your chances of effective speed reading by ensuring that you are reading in an environment conducive to efficient reading: for most of us this is a quiet place, free from disturbances (such as email, phone/text/IM, the television, radio or other people) but some people have reported the benefit of having low-level music (preferably instrumental rather than with lyrics) in the background as a way to help them focus.

It is also often more effective to read a section in the book or case report and then write notes about the main points at the end of the section rather than writing at the same time as reading (and therefore simply copying out the whole book in your own words). It may help to maximise your reading speed, and also your note-taking efficiency.

You may then wish to adopt one of a range of speed-reading techniques. Some people skim read, by running their eyes over the text very quickly with the aim of drawing out material on key points. For example, if you were reading a piece of academic commentary and you wanted to find material relevant to your assessment on parliamentary supremacy, you would scan each page for the words 'parliamentary supremacy' and when you come across them you would read the sentence before, the sentence containing the phrase and any related sentences subsequent to the phrase and make notes only on that material. You would not read the whole page, and you may find that you could skip whole pages at a time as none of them contain the phrase you are looking for. You could do a 'find' search for the phrase, if the document is an electronic one. This technique works very well for reading and note-taking related to assessments, as you already have background knowledge, and you are searching for evidence or authority to develop and to support your arguments. It works less well for textbook reading when you are trying to get to grips with a topic for the first time following a lecture. Another speed-reading technique is known as guiding, in which you use your finger, or another pointing aid, to move at speed underneath each of the words so that you do not dwell on each word too long and you encourage your eyes to keep moving forward rather than back and forth. There is some evidence to suggest that this is particularly helpful for some dyslexics and may increase their reading speed.

Another speed technique is known as chunking. This requires you to read chunks of material as a single unit, and to focus your eyes on the middle part of each phrase, allowing your subconscious to pick up the start and end of the sentence without being aware that you are reading it. This technique takes a little practice: some people find it helpful to practise reading in this way after first drawing two lines down a page (draw the first line so that it cuts off the first couple of words from each line, and the second line so that it does something similar with the end of the line) so that the page is divided into three. Focus your attention on the middle portion of the page and read by directing your eyes there. Consider whether you can gain an understanding quickly of what the author is saying using this approach. Once you are competent at this, move to stage two, which is to draw only one line down the centre of the page and to focus your attention either side of this line. Are you able to glean the essential information that way too? If so your reading speed should be up to three times faster than using standard reading techniques. You may still need to pause and read some sentences in full, but you may find this helps to locate sentences that are pertinent to your assessment or written task. There are some online tutorials on the internet that you may wish to try, were you to want to take this method further.

In the previous section on taking notes in lectures I gave examples of linear note-taking and Cornell note-taking but also suggested that you consider spider diagrams or flow charts too (examples of which can be found on the companion website). These note-taking techniques are transferable to textbooks, journal articles, official reports, cases and legislation too. But it may help to run through some of the key issues when reading and taking notes from different types of frequently used sources.

5.8.1 NOTE-TAKING FROM LEGAL SOURCES (CASES AND LEGISLATION)

When reading cases and legislation you need to be clear on your purpose as this will affect your approach. Are you reading so as to augment your understanding of how the case or the legislation supports a point that someone else has already made (a lecturer, a textbook writer) or are you reading so as to gather evidence that you can use to apply to a factual scenario such as a problem question? Or are you reading so that you understand the relevance of the case or the meaning of legislation more generally?

If your reading is more general in nature you may wish to refer to the case-note template and the legislation template on the companion website, at www.routledge.com/cw/webley, to guide your reading and note-taking in this regard. Cases are an important part of the study of law. They are evidence of what the law is. You do need to read cases and to know their ratio and any important points made by judges in their *obiter dicta*. It will be sufficient for most cases to have a basic understanding of the facts as well as an understanding of the legal reasons for the decision – why in legal terms X won the case and Y lost the case. Legislation is also fundamental, of course. It is rare that you need to know the detail of the whole statute, but it is important to know its general purpose (usually set out in the long title), its extent (to which parts of the UK does the statute apply; refer to the extent section towards the end), when it came into force, and then to understand the detail of the sections that you are focusing on. It is less usual for students to be asked to read a piece of legislation without also being asked to read for a particular purpose. But if you have been asked to do so you may want to look at the legislation template on the companion website to guide your reading and note-taking.

When reading to augment your understanding about how a particular case is evidence in support of a point that has been made by someone else, you may wish to focus on the *ratio* of the case and relevant *obiter* comments and use skimming techniques. You may want to first read the headnote, then the leading judgment, and then any key dissenting judgments. Your notes would focus on the judges' legal reasoning vis-à-vis the point or points that you are seeking to understand rather than provide a case-note-style summary. You may need to quote key passages, as these may become evidence for a point that you are making at a later stage, but try to summarise in your own words when quoting is not essential. When reading to augment your understanding about how a piece of legislation is evidence for a point that has been made, skim through the legislation to the point at which the particular issue is mentioned (the legislation may be organised into named parts that indicate the subject of the part) and then read the sections within that part, paying particular attention to those sections which set the parameters for the legal principle and those that provide restrictions on the application of the legal principle that follow. You will want to note down the essential elements of the legal principle (a flow diagram may help you with this). Ensure that in all instances you keep a full and accurate citation/reference of the source so that you can cite this in your written work. Refer to your English Legal System notes, or an English Legal System text if you are in any doubt about the operation of precedent, or the anatomy of primary and secondary legislation. I give some suggestions about relevant texts in the bibliography.

Reading and note-taking so as to help you with a problem question are a hybrid of the two other approaches above. You may first need to read the case or legislation so as to work out what it means, and you may then need to reread it having looked back at the facts in the problem question and worked out what you need to demonstrate in order for your client to be successful. Your first read through will be for meaning; the second read through will be to gather detailed evidence (which may well be quoted material) that you can use in order to reach a professional opinion and provide advice to your client. Refer back to Chapter 3 if you need to review how to use evidence in support of the points you are making in a problem scenario.

5.8.2 NOTE-TAKING FROM OTHER SOURCES

We have already covered reading and note-taking as regards textbooks (in the section on integrating your lecture notes and textbook notes). Suffice it to say that if you are reading to gain a more developed understanding of a topic then you are reading and note-taking so as to obtain the key principles, plus a small amount of detail associated with those principles so as to understand what they mean and what evidence there is in support of them. You may wish to use the guiding technique to speed up your reading. You could also use skimming or chunking but these may be less useful if you need to develop your understanding of an area rather than pick out key points which you have already identified as pertinent; chunking or skimming may work well if you have already attended a lecture on the topic and if you reread your lecture notes before you begin your textbook reading. The same rules apply to note-taking for this type of source: keep a full and accurate citation/reference for each source and for each piece of evidence that backs up a particular point, even if you summarise this material in your own words (refer to Chapter 6 if you are unsure how to do this); make notes with a purpose rather than trying to summarise everything that the writer has said. You may need to read a passage, think about what it means, reread it if necessary, put it to one side and then summarise the essence of that passage in one or two sentences. Alternatively you could adopt the Cornell note-taking approach and separate the key principle, and a (brief) explanation of the key principle including the evidence that supports it. Your notes should be considerably shorter than the text that you are reading.

You may also need to read journal articles, which are usually eight-to-ten-thousand-word pieces written by academics for academics. Consequently they are complex and can be challenging to read. But they are an extremely good source to use to examine what are the current (or historic) debates about a particular legal issue, what solutions we may have to deal with a problem, how the practice of law sheds light on the theoretical underpinnings or purpose of the law, etc. Academic articles give you a much deeper understanding of a subject area, although you may find them difficult to read to begin with. They are particularly useful if you are writing essays rather than problem questions. You should aim to read one article on each tutorial subject area to deepen your knowledge, but only after you have completed your textbook and case reading. Again, it is important to read and make notes with purpose. Consequently, your notes should be angled towards the key arguments, with some detail that provides the evidence in support of the key points.

You may have been set an article to read for a tutorial so as to answer a question. Check whether the tutorial question is asking you to read with a particular focus, and if so read and take notes for that purpose rather than taking more general notes. Consider reading the introduction and then the conclusion, before you move on to the main body of the article. You may find it helps you to identify the issues that you have been asked to focus on. Then use one of the speed-reading techniques for the main body of the article, and note down key issues and evidence (with references/citations) so that you may answer the tutorial question effectively. This approach may also help when reading an article you have identified as potentially relevant to an assessment question.

It is also possible that you have been asked to read a journal article to develop your knowledge of a topic. First read back through your existing lecture and textbook notes so that you are as clear as you can be on the topic, then move on to the article. One reading and note-taking approach would be to attempt to summarise each paragraph in one or two sentences, as above for textbook reading, then to read through those brief summaries and write a brief overview of what you think the article is arguing and concluding. Again, this task is likely to be easier if you have read the introduction (the signpost) and the conclusion (the thesis) before you begin reading the main body of the article. You may be able to use subheadings within the article to structure your notes. Keep a full reference/citation as before.

 More guidance is provided on reading and note-taking on the companion website.

5.9: ORGANISE YOUR IDEAS

- Read through all your notes and collate your information into themes, key principles or issues. You may find that diagrams help you, either to collate information or to clarify the essential features of the legal principle that is relevant to your client's case.

- Return to the question and review your information.

- Organise the themes to assist in planning your essay or problem question answer.

- Make sure that you include the evidence that relates to these themes, principles or issues.

Collate your information by reading through all your notes again and pulling together the themes you identify. Write down each one with any discussion you have found, as well as the sources you have referred to. Return to the question and consider the themes you have from your notes. What do these themes tell you as regards the question? What issues are relevant to the question and why? What evidence do you have for your thoughts about relevant issues? Evidence may be in the form of judicial opinion from a case, sections from a statute or other piece of legislation or the views of a commentator – academic or practitioner – or other relevant spokesperson. In some instances it may also be a worked example that shows what happened in a given situation. Organise the evidence under each theme ready to begin your writing. Write a brief comment about what the evidence means in relation to the theme and how this helps you to answer your question. You will make use of all of this material to construct paragraphs around your points. You may want to refer back to Chapter 2 on essay writing and Chapter 3 on problem questions so as to help with your planning phase.

5.10: MAKE SURE YOU REFERENCE THE WORK OF OTHERS

What is a reference/citation?

It is attributing the work that belongs to someone else to which you refer in your essays and presentations.

Why?

It should be possible from your references/citations for someone else to go to look up your evidence (from the case/legislation/journal article etc.) and read it in its original source.

You need to take down the reference/citation of any source you will use as part of your writing so that you are able to provide a reference to it in your written work. A full reference/citation will include the number of the page from which you have taken the information, so write this down at the time you are doing the research next to any notes you are making, otherwise you will have to go back to the library to try to find it before you can hand your work in.

Making Use of Evidence in Your Writing

- When you use evidence (usually in the form of what has been written or said by others) you demonstrate your skill or lack of skill as a scholar or legal professional.

- You should provide as much evidence as you reasonably can, to back up the points that you are making. Your aim is to persuade the reader that you are right in your analysis.

- However, try to describe the evidence in as little detail as you can, in order to justify your point effectively.

- **Always provide a full reference/citation for your evidence.**

- **Always introduce the point that you want to make first, before providing the evidence in support of the point.**

- **Finally, sum up your point at the end of your paragraph, so that the reader understands the final conclusion that you have reached, in the light of your evidence.**

It is difficult to underestimate the importance of your use of evidence in an assessment. A 2.2 answer can jump to a very high 2.1 answer, if sufficient evidence is used to add depth to arguments and authority and justification to the points being made. Thus, good research and note-taking are really important phases in excellent work. There are some examples on the companion website that illustrate this point. But it is also important to make sure that when you use evidence, you do so either in the form of quotes or as a paraphrased section. This means that you must either properly quote from the source to which you refer, and provide a full reference/citation to demonstrate its origin, or you must summarise the section that you are reading in your own words and then provide a full reference to the source, including the source's name. The next chapter will take you through this in more detail.

Next steps:

- You may wish to review your approach to research. How do you usually conduct research for essays and research for problem question answers? Consider the following:

  - How systematic is your approach to research?

  - How knowledgeable are you about the research resources that your university holds? Have you looked at any of the library research guides?

  - How much use do you make of primary sources of law?

  - How much use do you make of secondary, authoritative, sources?

  - Do you check the authority of secondary sources from the internet before you use them?

- Next, think about how you take notes from the sources that you have located. How much do you focus your notes on the question posed? Or do you tend to take general notes, many of which you do not use in your assessments?

- To what extent are you clear on when you are quoting someone's words, or summarising them entirely in your own words (paraphrasing)? Do you always note down full and accurate citations? You may wish to read the next chapter if you are in doubt about how to do this properly.

- You may also wish to undertake the library familiarity task to prepare yourself for your next assessment.

- There are more resources on the companion website to help you.

5.11: PREPARATION PRIOR TO YOUR RESEARCH: LIBRARY FAMILIARITY

You may find it useful to familiarise yourself with your law library and research sources before you begin your research. Pick up copies of your library's guidance leaflets, watch your library's introductory vodcast or work your way through the following task to familiarise yourself with the sources of information available to you and where they are located.

5.11.1 TEXTBOOKS

What subjects are you studying this year? Where would you find textbooks for those subjects in the library? Where would you find study guides and skills books to help you with your skills development? Are they held in hard copy or are they e-books that you access via your e-library portal?

5.11.2 LAW REPORTS

What law reports does your library hold? Which ones are only available in bound volumes on the shelves? Which are available in electronic format? Through which electronic databases do you access them (Westlaw, Lexis, Lawtel, etc.)?

5.11.3 LEGISLATION

Where can you find copies of *Halsbury's Statutes, Halsbury's Statutory Instruments* and the *Official Journal*? Do you have access to these sources in electronic form in your university and if so what do you need to do to be able to access these sources? Consider bookmarking online sites such as www.legislation.gov.uk so that you may access legislation quickly when you need it.

5.11.4 JOURNALS

What journals does your library subscribe to? Where are they located? Which ones are available in electronic form? How do you search them for relevant articles? Are you able to undertake a Google Scholar search (while logged in to your university account) so that you can click through via your e-library to gain access to relevant journal articles to which your university has subscribed?

5.11.5 OTHER LIBRARY SOURCES AND SERVICES

What other sources of information are available in your library? How do you access them? Is training provided for you in the use of the databases and search facilities and how do you go about getting the training you need?

SUMMARY

You may find that you can save time on research and find relevant material, by following these key stages in the research process.

> Identify the task set in the question, by dissecting it word for word. Identify keywords.

> Carry out background research if necessary, to ensure that you understand the question. This should usually include reading through any lecture and tutorial notes on the topics covered by the question. Refine keywords.

> Carry out textbook reading on the topic, making notes relevant to the question. Further refine keywords.

> Carry out research using the library catalogue to find any other texts relevant to the question. Make any additional notes that are relevant.

> Research cases and legislation that are relevant to the question and read important ones in full.

Research academic opinion on the topic by reading journal articles or academic texts and make notes on any issues raised that are relevant to the question.

Read through all the notes that you have made and make a list of key issues from your notes that are relevant to answering the question.

Highlight any evidence you have in your notes in support of or against the key issues you will discuss in your essay.

Make sure that you keep a record of all the sources you have used including the page references of the material you have noted down.

Turn this information into a plan, as discussed in Chapters 2, 3 and 4.

Begin writing your assessment.

6 CORRECT REFERENCING

Excellent academic written work is littered with research evidence, as discussed in the previous chapter. Referencing and citing others' work (along with primary legal sources such as legislation and cases) is one way of demonstrating your scholarly research skills. It demonstrates the wealth of material that you have found during your research phase. It also provides authority and weight to your arguments and allows you to justify your points and to persuade the reader or marker that your analysis is robust. In short, it is a very good thing. Some students think it is better to pretend that they have come up with an idea than to show that they have got the idea from something they have read. In fact, the opposite is true. Excellent work proudly shows off the sources that have been used in the writing process. In contrast, poor work provides few sources, but instead claims originality. Few academics will come up with a new original theory in their lifetime, and so we hardly expect undergraduates to do so. Even if you do manage to come up with a new theory, we will still expect it to be built on solid (research) foundations. In this chapter we shall address the nuts and bolts of how to reference or cite others' work. But first we shall deal with a related issue: quoting and paraphrasing.

Why have I included quoting and paraphrasing in this chapter? It could have been placed in the previous one, but equally it fits well with referencing issues. There are two main options when you read something that is relevant to your essay or problem question and you wish to refer to it in your own work. You may either quote the relevant passage, or you may paraphrase it. The difference is as follows:

> **Quoting** – Copying word for word what someone else has written and enclosing the passage in quotation marks, providing a reference to the original source.
>
> **Paraphrasing** – Reading what someone else has written. Putting the source to one side (so that you do not inadvertently copy it) and then summarising the essence of what they have said entirely in your own words. Then providing a reference to the original source.

When should you quote, and when should you paraphrase? The general rule of thumb is that you should only quote when it is essential for the reader to see the exact words that you have read (for example, a statement made by a judge in a case, or the wording of a piece of legislation). A quote should not be used as a way to avoid working out what a commentator is saying and summarising that point using your own words. It is also important to bear in mind that quotations may be good evidence to support a proposition you are making, but they are no substitute for developing your own analysis (something that you have worked out for yourself).

If you are referring to the words of others, you must indicate that the words belong to someone else by putting them in quotation marks in your text and providing a reference to where you found them, usually in a footnote or an endnote. You should also explain how the quote (the evidence) demonstrates that the point that you are making is correct.

A quote would be displayed as follows:

> 'Political sovereignty refers to the supreme political authority within a state. Legal sovereignty – from the standpoint of sovereignty within the state as opposed to sovereignty as understood in international law – refers to the supreme legal authority within a state.'[1]

Quotes of more than three or four lines long are usually indented and put on a separate line from the rest of the paragraph, as above. Shorter quotes would normally be set in the paragraph as normal. All quotes would normally be displayed with quotation marks. The usual form is to use '…' (single quotes or 'speech' marks) as quotation marks and then "…" (double quotes or 'quotation' marks) inside the first set of quotation marks, but few lecturers will be too worried about the type of quotation marks you use as long as you stick to a consistent style. Check with your lecturer to find out whether there is a style guide if you are unsure, particularly in respect of longer pieces of coursework such as dissertations. And if your university uses Turnitin anti-plagiarism software you may be asked to use single ('speech') marks rather than double ('quotation') marks as this makes a difference as to how the software identifies quotations.

It is not often necessary to use quotations, because the point being made by your source may be better and more concisely made by you. Paraphrasing is really the means by which you summarise the essence of what someone else has said, in clear and concise terms. However, this is also something that many students struggle with, because they often say that the original author said it better

---

1 For a more elaborate categorisation, see Rees, 'The theory of sovereignty restated', in Laslett, 1975, Chapter IV as cited in H. Barnett *Constitutional and Administrative Law* (11th edn, Routledge, 2015) p. 116.

in their own words. This may be true to an extent, but it often masks the real problem, which is that the student does not fully understand the phrase that they wish to use. It is hard to summarise something that one does not properly understand. You may need to give some thought to what the writer is trying to say (they may not have expressed themselves very clearly) and you may need to look up some of the words before you can summarise the phrase using your own language. But one of the benefits of paraphrasing someone else's words is that you get more credit for having taken the time to get to grips with the idea (whereas you only get credit for finding and using a quote). You can also explain the idea in concise terms and so save some words on an assessment with a tight word limit. But paraphrasing does need to be done properly, meaning that you need to use your own words rather than just changing a few words in the original passage. Failure to do so may lead to a charge of poor scholarship or, worse still, plagiarism. As a result, some students avoid paraphrasing like the plague. But paraphrasing is a skill like any other, and it is relatively easy to learn. Here are some examples of well-paraphrased and poorly paraphrased passages:

> **Original passage taken from H. Barnett *Constitutional and Administrative Law* 11th edn (Abingdon: Routledge, 2015) p. 121 para 1**
>
> **Parliament may also legislate with retrospective effect, as with the War Damage Act 1965. The War Damage Act effectively overruled the decision of the House of Lords in *Burmah Oil Company v Lord Advocate* (1965). In 1942, British troops had destroyed oil installations in Rangoon, with the intention of preventing them from falling into the hands of the Japanese. The British government made an *ex gratia* payment of some £4 million to the company. Burmah Oil sued the government for some £31 million in compensation. The House of Lords held that compensation was payable by the Crown for the destruction of property caused by the exercise of the prerogative power in relation to war. The government immediately introduced into Parliament the War Damage Bill to nullify the effect of the decision.**

An example of good paraphrasing would look like this:

> **Parliamentary supremacy permits parliament to legislate in any terms. It may even pass legislation that has retrospective effect, even if that means, as is the case of *Burmah Oil Company v. Lord Advocate* (1965), this effectively renders a court decision ineffective.[1]**
>
> 1 H. Barnett, *Constitutional and Administrative Law* (11th edn, Routledge, 2015) p. 116.

This passage summarises the main arguments accurately and succinctly. It does so in the author's own words rather than by using most of the same words from Barnett's original passage. It leaves out the description that is not needed to make the point, but it does provide the legal evidence in support of the point. There is also a full and accurate citation to demonstrate that this is Barnett's work paraphrased, rather than the student's own ideas. However, an example of poor paraphrasing would look something like this:

> **Parliament may also legislate retrospectively, as seen with the War Damage Act 1965. The War Damage Act overruled the decision of the House of Lords in *Burmah Oil Company v. Lord Advocate* (1965). In 1942 British troops destroyed oil installations in Rangoon, because they wanted to prevent them from falling into the hands of the Japanese. The British government made a payment of around £4 million to Burmah Oil. Burmah Oil sued the government for £31 million. The House of Lords held that the Crown had to pay compensation for the destruction of property caused by the use of the prerogative power in relation to war. The government immediately introduced the War Damage Bill to nullify the decision.[1] This is evidence of parliamentary supremacy in operation.**
>
> 1 H. Barnett *Constitutional and Administrative Law* (11th edn, Routledge, 2015), p. 116.

This passage is copied virtually word for word from Barnett's original text. However, as it is not included in quotation marks, the student is suggesting that the words are entirely her own. This passage either needed to be a proper summary of Barnett's ideas, in the student's own words, or an accurate quotation of them instead. This would likely be marked down for poor scholarship. The student has at least provided a full reference to Barnett's work, so there does not appear to be an attempt to deceive the reader into believing that the ideas are the student's own. But the student has given the impression that she has written this passage herself, when it is clear to us that she has really only edited Barnett's original text rather than summarising it herself.

Worse still is the next example, which is an out-and-out example of plagiarism. The student has copied sections of Barnett's work without enclosing them in quotation marks, or providing a reference to the source of the words or ideas.

> Parliament may also legislate with retrospective effect as with the War Damage Act 1965. The War Damage Act overruled the decision of the House of Lords in *Burmah Oil Company v. Lord Advocate* (1965). In 1942 British troops had destroyed oil installations in Rangoon, with the intention of preventing them from failing into the hands of the Japanese. The British government made an ex gratia payment of £4 million to the company. Burmah Oil sued the government for £31 million in damages. The House of Lords held that compensation had to be paid by the Crown for the destruction of property caused by the exercise of the prerogative power in relation to war. The government quickly introduced into parliament the War Damage Bill to nullify the effect of the decision. This is evidence of parliamentary supremacy in operation.

This would be taken very seriously. And in addition to the issue of plagiarism, the student has thrown away the opportunity to show off her research skills and the evidence that she has to support what she could have said had she taken the trouble to do so. So there are two issues here: first, has the student properly quoted or paraphrased the evidence that she is relying upon? And second, has she provided a full and accurate reference to the sources of those words or ideas (the evidence)? We have addressed the first of these, so we shall now turn our attention to the second.

Many students get very concerned about being found guilty of an assessment offence such as plagiarism, as academics are increasingly preoccupied with the problem of plagiarism and are stressing the importance of correct referencing in legal writing. Referencing can be a confusing business to begin with, but there are some simple rules that may help you with your writing and referencing, to make sure you steer clear of trouble. Put simply, referencing is giving credit to the author who had the idea or wrote the words that you are making use of in your essay or problem question answer. There are two broad schools, or ways of referencing: one known as Harvard (also sometimes called in-text referencing) and the other called Oxford (also sometimes known as numeric). Harvard-style referencing provides a brief reference to the author and his or her work at the end of the relevant sentence, followed by full citations at the end of the written work in endnotes or a bibliography. Oxford referencing makes use of footnotes instead. You can see examples of both on the companion website. The OSCOLA guide (it stands for Oxford Standard for Citation of Legal Authorities) is a particularly helpful and comprehensive guide on how to cite UK, EU and international legal sources.[2] The remainder of this chapter will focus on domestic legal sources, and so you may wish to

---

2 You can find it online at https://www.law.ox.ac.uk/research-subject-groups/publications/oscola.

consult the OSCOLA guide for non-UK ones as these are not addressed in detail here. The OSCOLA guidelines were updated in 2012 and this chapter reflects that updated guidance on references and citations.

6.1: WHAT IS REFERENCING?

> **It is attributing the work that belongs to someone else and which you are using in your written work or visual or oral presentations.**
>
> **It should be possible for someone else to look up the other person's work and read it in its original source after looking at your references.**
>
> **If you do not reference properly you may either be found to have undertaken *poor scholarship*, which will lose you considerable marks, or you may be found guilty of *plagiarism*, which has serious penalties attached.**

Many of the points that you make in your writing will be points that have been made previously by other people. That is the nature of undergraduate study and it shows that you have carried out research, for which you will receive credit. However, when you use someone else's idea or you use their words, you must also give that person credit by stating that the idea or words were theirs first. You may be found guilty of poor scholarship if you do not cite all your sources, for which you will lose marks, or you may be found guilty of plagiarism if it is considered that you set out to pretend that the idea or words were yours. Plagiarism can lead to very serious penalties, including expulsion from your course. A law school may be under a duty to disclose an offence to the Solicitors Regulation Authority and the Bar Standards Board, as is the student, which may make it difficult for them to become a member of the legal profession in later life. It is consequently important that you cite all your sources fully and accurately. In addition, good referencing may gain you marks.

In some places in this book I have used the words citing, citation or cite, and in others referencing, or reference. These two phrases are often used interchangeably but some law schools will use one and others will use the other. On that basis I have used both in this text, for the avoidance of doubt, and to ensure that it is clear that all material taken from any source must be attributed through the use of speech or quotation marks if quoted and whether quoted or paraphrased by use of a citation or reference at the end of each sentence that makes use of material from that source.

6.2: WHAT IS PLAGIARISM?

Plagiarism is taking (some would say *stealing*) others' words or ideas without stating whose words or ideas they are and where they came from.

It is not just a case of failing to put quotation marks around someone else's words.

It includes taking others' ideas, ones that you have not come up with yourself, and then not stating that they belong to someone else.

Paraphrasing others' words is only acceptable if you attribute those ideas to the person who thought of them.

In other words you should cite the other person's work if:

- You are quoting their words.

- You are paraphrasing their words by using their ideas but not their exact words (any ideas that you have not come up with yourself).

To be clear, plagiarism is taking someone else's words or someone else's ideas without stating the sources from which you got them. This would include taking a chunk of text from a book or an electronic source, including the internet, and putting it into your essay without adding speech or quotation marks around the words and without including a footnote stating the source of those words. It would include putting someone else's words into your own words (paraphrasing) and not adding a footnote stating from where these ideas originated. Students often say that they find it hard to know when to put a reference or footnote to another's source. The rule of thumb should be that you put a reference to the source whenever you have not come up with the idea you are discussing or the words you are using yourself. This means that most sentences and paragraphs will contain a number of references to others' work, although it is likely that the first sentence and last sentences are your own original work and will thus not need to be referenced/footnoted. Law schools usually ask you to put your references in footnotes and the OSCOLA guidelines indicate the use of footnotes over other forms of referencing. Some schools may ask you to use endnotes (similar to footnotes, but rather than the material appearing at the bottom of the page, it will appear in a section at the end of the document). Others may ask you to use in-text references (Harvard style), but that is relatively unusual and this chapter will thus focus on referencing via footnotes. You may want to double-check the school policy on this if you are unsure.

6.3: HOW TO REFERENCE

There are different ways of citing work; however, there are certain key pieces of information that a full reference must contain.

Adopt a consistent style and make sure you include all the relevant information.

Learn to use footnotes or endnotes if you have not used them before.[1]

---

1 A footnote generally appears at the bottom of the page (as this one does) and contains all the information that is necessary for the reader to find the original source. Word processing programmes such as Word have an 'add footnote' function in the menu on the toolbar.

There are some general rules about how you should display case names, statutory references and quotes from texts. Many of the rules are not hard and fast, but you do need to adopt a consistent style throughout your answer. We shall use the OSCOLA guidelines as these have been developed specifically for law, and they are the ones used by most law schools. But do be sure to comply with your own law school's policy on this. The general rules are set out below.

6.4: HOW TO REFERENCE BOOKS

OSCOLA guideline:

Author's name, *Title of the Book* (Edition, Place of Publication Publisher Year of publication), page number if relevant.

Note:

• the comma after the author's name;

• in bibliographies the author's surname comes first then the initial; in footnotes the author's first name or initials are first, then the surname;

• the comma after the book title, which is in italics;

• the inclusion of the edition within the bracket, followed by a comma;

• that the place of publication has now become optional information; and that the information within the bracket, with the exception of the edition, is separated by spaces but no other punctuation.

Refer to section 3 of the current OSCOLA guidelines for more detailed guidance.

Other styles you may see:

For example:
Webley, L. C., *Legal Writing* 4th edn (Abingdon: Routledge, 2016).

Or:
L.C. Webley (2016) *Legal Writing* 4th Edition (Abingdon: Routledge).

Or hybrids of those two styles.

A full reference for a book will include the name of the author, the title of the book, the edition of the book (if there is one), the place of publication of the book (now optional), the name of the publisher and the year of publication. This is enough information for the bibliography, but you will also need to provide a page reference for the source of your information in a footnote or endnote.

6.5: HOW TO REFERENCE JOURNAL ARTICLES

OSCOLA guideline for hard copy journals:

For journals with years only:
Author's name, 'Title of the Article' [year] Title of the Journal or official abbreviation first page number of the article and page number if needed to reference a quote or idea

For journals with years and volumes:
Author's name, 'Title of the Article' (year) Volume number Title of the Journal or official abbreviation first page number of the article and page number if needed to reference a quote or idea

Note:

the comma after the author's name;

in bibliographies the author's surname comes first, then the initial; in footnotes the author's first name or initials are first, then the surname;

- the article title in quotation marks;

- the type of brackets you need to use depending on whether the journal is indexed purely by year or by year and volume;

- the journal title or official abbreviation is now not italicised;

- the page number of the first page of the article; and

- the information within the bracket with the exception of the edition.

Refer to section 3 of the current OSCOLA guidelines for more detailed guidance.

OSCOLA guidelines for electronic journals:
Author's name, 'Title of the Article' [year] Title of the Journal or official abbreviation <web address> date accessed

Or
Author's name, 'Title of the Article' (year) Volume number Title of the Journal or official abbreviation <web address> date accessed

Other styles you may see:

For example:
Webley, L.C. 'Pro Bono and Young Solicitors: Views From the Front Line' Vol. 3 (2) (2000) *Legal Ethics* 152–168.

Or:
Webley, L.C. (2000) 'Pro Bono and Young Solicitors: Views From the Front Line' Vol. 3 (2) Legal Ethics 152–168.

Or a hybrid of these two.

A full reference for a journal article will include the name of the author, the title of the article (usually in quotation marks), the volume number and/or the year of the journal that the article appears in, the title of the journal and the starting page of the journal article. A full reference in a footnote would also include a reference to the page from which you have taken the idea or the quotation. Online journals are referenced in a similar way. It is not possible (usually) to provide a page reference but you should provide the web address and the date on which you access it. Web pages contain dynamic content which changes over time, so it is important to know when you accessed the material you are relying upon in your written work.

6.6: HOW TO REFERENCE CASES

OSCOLA guideline:

Cases without neutral citations:
Name of the case [year] Law Report abbreviations first page number, page reference for passage if needed

Or:
Name of the case (year) volume of the law report, Law Report abbreviations page, page reference for passage if needed

Case with neutral citations:
Name of the case [year] court number, [year] Law Report abbreviation first page number, page reference for passage if needed

Or:
Name of the case [year] court number (year) volume Law Report abbreviation first page number, page reference for passage if needed

Note:

- the case name should be in italics and the 'v' should be in italics but not be followed by a full stop;

- there is no punctuation in the citations (aside from spaces) other than in neutral citations when it appears between the neutral citation and the law report citations. Neutral citations are relatively new and most cases will be cited with a non-neutral citation;

- which type of brackets you need to enclose the year.

Other styles you may see:
Attorney-General v. Guardian Newspapers Ltd (No. 2) [1990] 1 AC 109

Or:
Attorney-General v. Guardian Newspapers Ltd (No. 2) [1990] 1 AC 109

Cases names should be *italicised* although some law schools may ask you to use **bold** or <u>underlining</u>. If you are writing by hand then they should be underlined. The case name should be written out in full (you only need write out the first claimant and first defendant if there are many parties involved in the case) unless you are writing an assessment under anything other than exam conditions. If you are writing an answer to a problem question in an exam and you have not been permitted to bring materials such as a notebook in with you, then the use of abbreviated forms of case names is usually acceptable. You are permitted to shorten commonly named parties or phrases, such as the Director of Public Prosecutions to the DPP. You are permitted to shorten case names in a work after the first time you have cited them in full, by using the name of the first named party in civil cases and using the name of the defendant in criminal cases. There is more information on this in the OSCOLA guidelines available online, including more detailed information on how to use neutral citations and how to cite cases from other jurisdictions.

6.7: HOW TO REFERENCE STATUTES

> **OSCOLA guideline:**
>
> **Short Title of the Act Year of Enactment sections to which you refer, if needed**
>
> **Note:**
>
> • the short title of the Act is in title case (capital letters at the start of major words) and standard typeface (roman);
>
> • there is no comma between the title of the Act and the year of enactment;
>
> • if you refer to sections you may write 'section' or 'sections' or abbreviate these to 's' or 'ss' but do not use a full stop after the 's'.
>
> **Refer to section 2 of the current OSCOLA guidelines for more detailed guidance.**
>
> **Other styles you may see:**
>
> **Human Rights Act 1998 s 1 (indicating section 1) Human Rights Act 1998 ss 1–6 (indicating sections 1–6)**

Statute names should be displayed in full the first time you use them, but as long as you provide a definition, they may then be cited in abbreviated format thereafter; the abbreviation would normally be the letters from the main words in the title and should include the year. An example of a statute displayed in traditional form is set out above. If you wish to use an abbreviation for all sub-sequent mentions of the Act then please define the abbreviation when you provide the full citation as so:

'Human Rights Act (HRA) 1998, hereafter cited as HRA 1998.'

Remember too that whenever you refer to the 'Act', the 'A' should be capitalised thus:

'The Act came into force on 2nd October 2000.'

If you are citing particular sections of an Act then you may write 'section' or abbreviate it to 's'.

'The Human Rights Act 1998 s 6 states that…'

If you are referring to multiple sections then you would cite them by doubling the 's':

'The Human Rights Act 1998 ss 6–8 indicates that…'

If you are unsure then it is always safer to go with the long version, to write out the word 'section' than to make up an abbreviation.

There is more information on this in the OSCOLA guidelines available online, including more detailed information on how to refer to secondary legislation and legislation from other jurisdictions.

6.8: HOW TO REFERENCE WEB PAGES

OSCOLA guideline:

Citations as above (for books, journal articles, etc.) or equivalent <web address> date accessed

Note:

- **you should only cite the electronic copy if it is not published in hard copy form; if it is published in hard copy form cite the hard copy;**

- **you must provide the full web address; you do not need the http:// prefix unless the web address does not begin with www;**

- cite the most recent date on which you accessed the web page as 'accessed 7 November 2015';

- there is no comma between the title of the Act and the year of enactment.

Refer to more detailed guidance in section 3 of the current OSCOLA guidelines.

Other styles you may see:
Syrett, K. 'Of resources, rationality and rights: emerging trends in the judicial review of allocative decisions.' [2000] 1 *Web JCLI* at http://webjcli.ncl.ac.uk/2000/issue1/syrett1.html accessed on 25 June 2004.

Web page citations follow the citation conventions set out for books or articles for the first part of the citation, but then also include a full reference to the web page at which the article can be found as well as the date on which you accessed it. You should include the date as web page content is dynamic and changes rapidly. Errors could have been corrected since you accessed the page, or alternatively the article could have been replaced or removed altogether. By including the date you are more protected from the charge that you have incorrectly cited information. Please note, however, that if the publication is available in hard copy form then you should cite the hard copy version.

6.9: How to Reference Edited Collections

OSCOLA guideline:

Author's name, 'Title of the Chapter' in editor's name (ed.), *Title of the Book* (Edition, Place of Publication Publisher Year of publication), pages of the chapter, page number for specific passage in the chapter if relevant.

Note:

- the comma after the author's name;

- in bibliographies the author's surname comes first, then the initial; in footnotes the author's first name or initials are first, then the surname;

- the chapter title is in quotation marks;

- the editor's name is preceded by in and followed by (ed.) (or eds if more than one editor) and a comma;

- the comma after the book title, which is in italics;

- the inclusion of the edition within the bracket followed by a comma, if needed;

- that the place of publication has now become optional information; and

- that the information within the bracket, with the exception of the edition, is separated by spaces but no other punctuation.

Refer to section 3 of the current OSCOLA guidelines for more detailed guidance.

Other styles you may see:

For example:
McGlynn, C. 'Judging Women Differently: Gender, The Judiciary and Reform' in Millns, S. and Whitty, N. (eds) *Feminist Perspectives on Public Law* (London: Cavendish Publishing, 1999) pp. 87–106

Or:
McGlynn, C. (1999) 'Judging Women Differently: Gender, The Judiciary and Reform' in Millns, S. and Whitty, N. (eds) *Feminist Perspectives on Public Law* (London: Cavendish Publishing) pp. 87–106

Or a hybrid of these styles.

Edited collections are hybrids of journal article and book citations. You should include the name of the author of the chapter, the title of the chapter in quotation marks, the names of the editors, the title of the book in italics, the place of publication, the publisher and the year of publication. Foot-noted sources should also include the page number from which the source originates.

6.10: How to Reference Others' References

> **You must cite all sources of information including the source that your source is citing.**
>
> **If your source refers to someone else's source then cite both:**
>
> **For example:**
> **Dicey (1885), p. 39 as cited in Barnett, H. *Constitutional and Administrative Law* 7th edn (London: Routledge-Cavendish, 2008) at p. 133.**
>
> **In the example, Barnett is my source but I want to refer to Dicey, to whom Barnett refers and whom she cites in her work.**

To avoid a charge of plagiarism you must be sure to cite your sources (the book or article that you have read) as well as the source of the original information. This sounds complicated but is actually quite easy. Your source is your reference point and the reader needs to know from where you got the information. The source of the original information is the source that your textbook writer or other author mentions. Your footnote needs to include all the information required to find the original source and your source. That way the reader may retrace your research steps and also those of the people who have done their own research to find the original source of the information.

6.10.1 USING ABBREVIATIONS IN FOOTNOTES AND ENDNOTES

Students tend to get rather worried about how to use Latin abbreviations in footnotes. The new OSCOLA guidelines suggest that we use English equivalents in most cases rather than the Latin abbreviations, but you will see the Latin versions in many of the sources that you read, and so you will need to understand what they mean. Your law school may also ask you to make use of them. The OSCOLA guidelines are relatively open on how to abbreviate and refer to sources that you have cited in full early on in the work. They indicate that you should be able to identify the source: for a book you may use the author's name and indicate the footnote in which the full citation can be found (for example Webley (n5): this indicates that the full citation for Webley can be found in footnote 5) as well as including the page number for the passage or idea that you are citing from Webley's work. You may also use abbreviated case names or statutory names in the same way, but in compliance with the guidelines above on how you truncate these types of source. There is additional guidance in section 1 of the current OSCOLA guidelines, were you to want it. It is important to note that you should always write out the reference in full the first time you refer to an author's work. You may thereafter abbreviate the reference.

It is also worth including the full citation in every footnote until your final draft, as if you move the text around while redrafting your essay or problem answer the footnotes will change order too. Consequently, in the example above Webley (n5) may no longer be accurate as the first full citation of Webley may now be in a completely different footnote. This can be difficult to unravel, and so you may prefer to leave abbreviations until the final draft. Most markers will prefer to see abbreviated references for repeated citations in the final version of your assessment, as it is less cluttered and makes it easier to read.

Some academics still prefer to use Latin abbreviations instead of English ones. The traditional approach was that abbreviations should always end with a full stop as indicated below, although in more modern texts full stops are omitted to provide a less cluttered style and the OSCOLA guidelines indicate that we should omit full stops. The Latin abbreviations that you will see in your reading include the following:

Latin abbreviations

Latin abbreviations you may see during your research and reading, and which you may use in your essays, are:

Id.

Ibid.

Loc. cit.

Op. cit.

Supra

Id. – This means 'exactly the same as cited directly above' and is used if the footnote or endnote is exactly the same as the one immediately above it. It should be the same in all respects including the same page reference. In this instance the footnote would simply contain the abbreviation '*id*.' Or '*Id*.'. Many people do not use '*Id*.' but instead use '*Ibid*.'

Ibid. – This means 'in exactly the same book as cited directly above' and is used if the footnote or endnote is exactly the same as the one immediately above this one, but for a different page number. In this instance the footnote would be displayed thus:

1. A.H. Sherr and L.C. Webley, 'Legal Ethics in England and Wales' (1997) Vol. 4 Nos. 1/2 *International Journal of the Legal Profession* pp. 109–138.
2. *Ibid.* at p. 130, or *Ibid.* at 130, or *Ibid.* p. 130.

Loc. cit. – This means 'in the place that has been cited above' and is used where the full citation for a book, report or journal article has been provided previously in an earlier footnote or endnote, including the page reference or the paragraph. It is similar to '*id.*' but for the fact that there are other footnotes or endnotes in between the original citation and the current one. In traditional works this form of abbreviation is not used for cases or for legislation, which should be cited in full in each instance; however, the rule is becoming blurred.

3. A.H. Sherr and L.C. Webley, *loc. cit.* at note 1.

Op. cit. – This means 'in the work cited above' and is used where the full citation has been provided in an earlier footnote or endnote above, but not in the footnote immediately above this one. *Op. cit.* relates to books, reports and journal articles but not to cases or to legislation. In order for the reader to know which source the writer refers to, the footnote should also contain the authors of the source and may include the footnote or endnote that contains the full citation as follows:

4. A.H. Sherr and L.C. Webley *op. cit.* at note 1 at p. 131.

This could be displayed in a more simplified form as follows:

4. Sherr and Webley, *op. cit.* at 131, or 4. Sherr and Webley, *op. cit.* at p. 131.

Supra – This means 'above' and is used where the full citation has been provided previously in an earlier footnote or endnote. It would normally be followed by the footnote number that contains the full citation as well as the page number relevant to the current footnote. *Supra* is often used in essays in place of both *loc. cit.* and *op. cit.*

There are others, but these are the most commonly used in legal academic writing.[3] An English equivalent to the Latin versions would simply be to write

3 For a fuller discussion of Latin abbreviations and their use in footnotes and endnotes see E. Campbell and R. Fox, *Students' Guide to Legal Writing and Law Exams* (2nd edn, The Federation Press 2003).

'As above' followed by the identifying information that follows the Latin abbreviations in the examples above.

6.11: BIBLIOGRAPHIES VS. FOOTNOTES/ ENDNOTES

A bibliography is used at the end of a piece of legal writing. It sets out all the sources to which you personally referred.

Footnotes appear at the bottom of each page and they contain the sources you referred to as well as any sources that you are referring to which your own source also referred to (as set out above).

Endnotes are similar to footnotes but they all appear at the end of the piece of legal writing, although they are numbered in the text in ways similar to footnotes.

Some lecturers may ask you to use footnotes, or to use endnotes. Some will require you to include a bibliography of your sources at the end of your writing as well as footnotes/endnotes; others will not require both. Check to see what the conventions are for each module. Note that if you are following the OSCOLA guidelines to the letter then you would need to change round the author's first name and last name as between the footnotes and the bibliography, as indicated above. Many markers will also want to see citations grouped by source, so all books together (and ordered alphabetically by the first author's last name, all journal articles similarly grouped, all cases together listed alphabetically, all legislation similarly, etc.).

 You will find more guidance in the OSCOLA guide, a link to which is to be found on the companion website.

To conclude, it is important that you reference your work fully. If in doubt, it is better to over-reference rather than to under-reference. Keep clear notes of your sources during the research phase, including the page numbers from which you have taken notes. It is often easier to photocopy the title page of the source you are using at the same time as you photocopy the pages to which you are going to refer, as this contains most of the information that you will need for your footnotes. Please ensure that any copying that you do falls within the Higher Education Copyright Licence Agreement (a copy of which is likely to be displayed near the university photocopiers or if not may be available from the library counter and is in any event available online). Your bibliography will include all sources that you have read and made use of in your written work.

Next steps:

- Check your written work carefully to make sure that you have either properly quoted or properly paraphrased others' work.

- Any idea or phrase that is not your own should be cited appropriately.

- Check too that you have properly referenced all your sources according to the Harvard or the Oxford (OSCOLA) methods of referencing (or your law school's own style).

- Check your bibliography to make sure that you have included any source that has helped to form your views in writing the answer. Do not include sources that you have not read personally.

- There are also some exercises to undertake to test your ability to reference and cite others' work, which you may wish to try. The answers are towards the back of the book.

- There are further exercises on citing and referencing on the companion website.

- You may wish to check your understanding of the difference between quoting and paraphrasing by visiting the companion website where you can test your knowledge.

6.12: TEST YOUR UNDERSTANDING OF REFERENCING: EXERCISE ONE – CITING OTHERS' WORK

Read the extract below from Hilaire Barnett's book then try the following task. There are answers set out at the back of the book.

6

PARLIAMENTARY SOVEREIGNTY[4]

...

INTRODUCTION

[1] Under any constitution – whether written or unwritten – there must be a source of ultimate authority: one supreme power over and above all other power in the state. Under a written constitution the highest source of power is the Constitution as interpreted by the Supreme Court. Under the British constitution, in theory if not in practice, the highest source of authority is the United Kingdom Parliament and Acts of Parliament are the highest form of law.

[2] Writing in the late nineteenth century, A.V. Dicey took the view that the supremacy of Parliament is 'the dominant characteristic of our political institutions'.[5] However, the concept of sovereignty has long caused controversy and is one which assumes differing interpretations according to the perspective being adopted. For example, international lawyers are concerned with the attributes which identify a state as independent and sovereign within the international community. Political scientists on the other hand are concerned with the source of political power within a state. From the perspective of legal theorists and constitutional lawyers the focus is on the ultimate legal power within a state.

To categorise Britain as a sovereign independent state with the ultimate source of legal authority vesting in its Parliament was accurate in the nineteenth century. However, in today's world of increasing economic legal and political interdependence the traditional theory of sovereignty has an air of unreality about it. International relations and obligations, membership of the European Union, devolution of law-making powers away from Westminster to Northern Ireland, Scotland and Wales and other factors all restrict what Parliament can in fact do: theory and practice are increasingly separated. In this chapter we examine the various aspects of sovereignty, and the challenges posed to the orthodox view.

---

4 Extract from H. Barnett, *Constitutional and Administrative Law* (11th edn, Routledge 2015) p. 116.
5 Dicey, 1885, p. 39.

LEGAL AND POLITICAL SOVEREIGNTY

Political sovereignty refers to the supreme political authority within a state. Legal sovereignty – from the standpoint of sovereignty within the state as opposed to sovereignty as understood in international law – refers to the supreme legal authority within a state.[6]

It is often difficult to distinguish clearly between legal and political sovereignty. The distinction is nevertheless one insisted upon by authorities such as Sir Edward Coke, Sir William Blackstone and AV Dicey. In large measure, this clear demarcation between the political and the legal is explained by the unwritten nature of the United Kingdom's constitution. In the majority of states having a written constitution, the constitution defines the limits of governmental power. In the United Kingdom, by way of contrast, the powers of government – whilst ultimately dependent upon the electoral 'mandate' – remain unconstrained by any fundamental written document and subject only to Parliament's approval. All law-making power thus derives, not from a power-conferring and power-delimiting constitutional document, endorsed by the people, but from the sovereignty of the legislature: Parliament.

[3] Social contract theory underpins the political sovereignty of the people. Two early theorists may briefly be considered here. In *Two Treatises on Government* (1690)[7] John Locke advances powerful arguments for the limits of governmental power and the ultimate political sovereignty of the people. Locke argues that men come together in civil society and tacitly consent to be ruled by government directed to 'the peace, safety and public good of the people'.[8] Accordingly, the power conferred on government is not absolute, but whilst in existence, is supreme power. However, Locke concludes that if the people: *[page 117 begins here]*

> ...have set limits to the duration of their legislative, and made this supreme power in any person or assembly only temporary, it is forfeited; upon the forfeiture of their rules, or at the determination of the time set, it reverts to the society, and the people have a right to act as supreme, and continue the legislative in themselves or place it in a new form, or new hands, as they think good.[9]

---

6 For a more elaborate categorisation, see Rees, 'The theory of sovereignty restated', in Laslett, 1975, Chapter IV.
7 Locke, 1977, Book II.
8 At p. 182.
9 At p. 242.

Sovereignty – the supreme power – is limited and conditional: government holds power on trust for the people.

1   Read the first paragraph marked with [1] and quote the first sentence. Provide a full reference in a footnote for the quote.
2   Read the paragraph marked with [2]. Put the main points in your own words (paraphrase them) in one paragraph of your own, as you would for an essay. Provide footnotes citing that work in full.
3   Read the paragraph marked with [3] and quote the quote that Barnett employs in that paragraph including the lead-in sentence. Provide a full reference including the primary and secondary source.

The answers are set out in the answer section towards the end of the book.

6.13: TEST YOUR UNDERSTANDING OF REFERENCING: EXERCISE TWO – FULL AND ACCURATE REFERENCING

Look at the following title pages and then write a full citation for each one. The answers are towards the back of the book.

FEMINIST PERSPECTIVES ON PUBLIC LAW

Cavendish
Publishing
Limited

London and Sydney

First published in Great Britain 1999 by Cavendish Publishing Ltd,
The Glass House, Wharton Street, London WC1X 9PX, United Kingdom
Telephone: +44 (0) 171 278 8000 Facsimile: + 44 (0) 171 278 8080
E-mail: info@cavendishpublishing.com
Visit our Home page on http://www/cavendishpublishing.com

Feminist perspectives on public law
I. Public law
II. Millns, S II. Whitty, Noel
342.4′1

ISBN 1 85841 480 X

Printed and bound in Great Britain

Extract from Contents Page:

cont...

Cite in full Thérèse Murphy's chapter in this edited collection.

CONSTITUTIONAL & ADMINISTRATIVE LAW

.... ELEVENTH EDITION ....

Hilaire Barnett

Routledge

Eleventh Edition published 2016
by Routledge
2 Park Square, Milton Park, Abingdon, Oxon OX14 4RN

and by Routledge
711 Third Avenue, New York, NY 10017

Routledge is an imprint of the Taylor & Francis Group, an informa business

First edition published by Cavendish Publishing 1995
Tenth edition published by Routledge 2013

British Library Cataloguing in Publication Data
A catalogue record for this book is available from the British Library

Library of Congress Cataloging-in-Publication Data
A catalog record for this title has been requested

ISBN: 978-1-138-81476-9 (pbk)
ISBN: 978-1-315-74724-8 (ebk)

Typeset in Joanna
by Wearset Ltd, Boldon, Tyne and Wear

Cite Hilaire Barnett's book in full as you would in a bibliography.

SUMMARY

Others' words and ideas must be fully and accurately referenced in your written work. Failure to reference properly may result in marks being deducted for poor scholarship, or a charge of plagiarism being made against you.

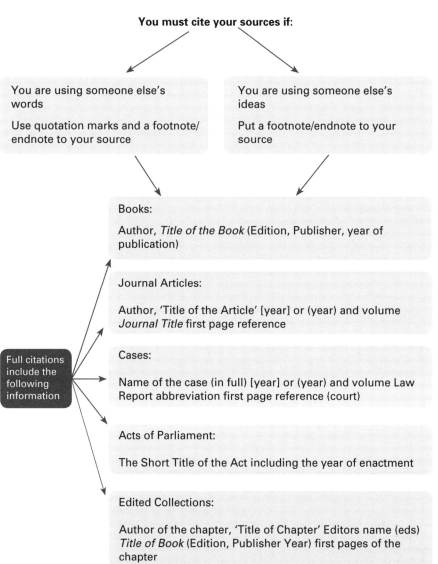

You must cite your sources if:

You are using someone else's words

Use quotation marks and a footnote/endnote to your source

You are using someone else's ideas

Put a footnote/endnote to your source

Full citations include the following information

Books:

Author, *Title of the Book* (Edition, Publisher, year of publication)

Journal Articles:

Author, 'Title of the Article' [year] or (year) and volume *Journal Title* first page reference

Cases:

Name of the case (in full) [year] or (year) and volume Law Report abbreviation first page reference (court)

Acts of Parliament:

The Short Title of the Act including the year of enactment

Edited Collections:

Author of the chapter, 'Title of Chapter' Editors name (eds) *Title of Book* (Edition, Publisher Year) first pages of the chapter

7

COMPLETING, POLISHING AND PRESENTING YOUR WORK

Essays and problem question answers are not just about the ideas that are contained within them, although they are obviously extremely important. They are also about communicating those ideas and the evidence you have to back up your assertions in an effective and stylish fashion. The way in which you communicate those ideas may be more or less persuasive to the reader. The more gaps you leave in your arguments, and the less clearly you express your ideas, the more likely it is that you will lose the reader and the chance to get your point across. This chapter considers the important stage of finishing and polishing your answer before handing it in to be marked. It provides some hints to help you make the most of your writing.

7.1: FINISHING AND POLISHING YOUR WRITTEN WORK

Finish what you consider to be the final draft of your essay.
Leave it alone for 24 hours.

Return to your essay.

Reread the question or problem and then reread your draft once through. Take note of the ideas and arguments in the draft.

Start at the beginning and ask yourself:

- 'Have I signposted my approach to the question in the introduction?'

- 'Have I answered the question?'

- 'Have I grouped together all aspects of each point in a single paragraph?'

- 'Do I need to rearrange the order of ideas so that they flow?'

- 'Have I explained where my arguments are going throughout the essay?'

> **Make any changes.**
>
> **Read the draft again to check individual paragraphs.**
>
> **Ask yourself for each paragraph:**
>
> - 'Have I stated the point that I am making/the conclusion that I have reached having analysed everything I read?'
>
> - 'Have I explained my point?'
>
> - 'Have I provided evidence to back up the point and explained how the evidence does so?'
>
> - 'Have I cited all my sources?'
>
> - 'Have I rounded off the point by explaining its relevance to the question and how it helps to answer to question?'
>
> **Reread one final time to check that:**
>
> - **Your spellings and grammar are correct.**
>
> - **Your essay looks professional.**

It is difficult to reflect on your own work, and particularly so if you complete your first draft and then move to polish and finish it straight away. Leaving a period of 24 hours between completing your pre-final draft and starting to polish it will allow the issues to settle in your mind. It will also make it easier to view your essay objectively, to read it as the marker will read it. Students tend to lose 'easy' marks by failing to polish their work. Spelling errors are avoidable (although I'll leave you to spot how many you can find in this book!), as are formatting problems, missing footnotes and poor editing mistakes. Just for fun, an example that would not be atypical would be something like this:

> *Parliamentary supremmacey is a theory of how what power Parliament has to legislate ... theorists such as Dicy have set out the basic tennents of the theory.*[1]

1

While the ideas contained in those two sentences would give a student some marks, they may equally have resulted in a drop of overall essay mark, because the essay was so badly finished. In addition, the citation is missing and the point is not fully made. Some of these issues can be picked up by a judicious proofread. Others are stylistic and require you to read your work with a critical eye and redraft, reread and redraft again. You may want to try the redrafting technique that I set out in the essay and problem question answer chapters, if you have not already done so. I suggested that to redraft your paragraph so as to develop analysis you should take your concluding sentence (if you have one) and place it at the top of the paragraph, then redraft the middle section of the paragraph so that it acts as a justification for why you are correct in your analysis (your conclusion). You will need to explain how the evidence (cases, statutes, etc.) acts as a justification rather than simply reporting on your evidence. You may then reread your paragraph and consider whether you are able to reach a higher level of analysis still (critical analysis) by explaining how your new insight is relevant or important as regards the question. Finally, consider how persuasive your paragraph is. Will you have convinced the reader that you are correct in your analysis? Do you need to provide more evidence, more justification and explanation or to make your point more crisply? And have you really weighed up all the evidence fairly so as to reach appropriate conclusions or have your sought to use the evidence to fit with your personal opinion? Remember that your scholarly opinion is distinct from your personal opinion. Your scholarly opinion must be formed having read the full range of views and balanced all the evidence, you should not seek out evidence that supports your personal opinion and then seek to persuade the reader that your view is right! Next, having redrafted elements of your answer consider whether this impacts on any of the rest of your answer, do you need to redraft others sections now too? And can you reorder your paragraphs or link them together so that your arguments flow more effectively or become more persuasive?

7.1.1 LINKING IDEAS INTO AN ARGUMENT

Once you have written your answer, it is important that you read through your draft with connections in mind. You may have assigned one paragraph per idea and you may have explained how the idea related to the question; however, it is difficult to link each of the ideas together in your essay at the same time as writing them down for the first time. Indeed, many academics would argue that strong written work may have been through as many as five drafts before it is complete (some of us consider many more may be needed). Most students, and indeed many academics, do not know what they think about a subject until they have either discussed the ideas or written them down and reworked them. Consequently, it is hard to develop and link ideas at the point when you are trying to get them down on paper. Instead, it is important to give yourself a break from your essay once the first draft is completed, to let the ideas settle in your mind for a day or so, and then to return to your draft to link those ideas together in your essay.

Linking ideas is simply a way of explaining how one idea fits with the next, so that the reader can develop a picture of how the ideas relate to one another and you can persuade them that your thesis (your conclusion) is robust. This is one of the hallmarks of good analysis. One of the easiest ways of doing this is to group those issues that appear to point to one answer in your essay – for example issues that appear to be in favour of a proposition in a title – and then move on to address those that appear to be against a proposition. You may wish to balance one paragraph, which argues in favour of one point of view, with a following paragraph that appears to contradict it, before moving on to the next theme on your list. This can work well, and has the benefit of simplicity, but if can also lead to a disjointed series of arguments that do not flow very well. Alternatively, you may wish to adopt a thematic approach in which you deal with all of the evidence related to one issue in a given paragraph. This allows you to weigh up the evidence and reach a nuanced conclusion. In turn that allows you to develop a clear point, which you can then justify by explaining the conflicting evidence and how you have reached your conclusion. This may take a little time to master, but if you do it is likely to be persuasive and yield good results. There are many different ways to link ideas, but the important part of argument construction is that the reader can follow the development of your ideas, rather than that you adopt a particular pattern. Further, you want to ensure that anything you have learned in a later paragraph is reflected, where relevant, in an earlier one. The answer should read as if you knew the answer before you started to write it rather than you discovered the answer as you went along. So links are important not just as regards flow, but also so as to develop critical analysis – analysis that builds on other analysis to present a nuanced critique in the light of all that you know.

Problem question answers should be structured so as to move logically through the legal issues that must be proved or disproved, met or not met, in order for the legal points to be settled. Some legal issues are prerequisites, and if these have not been met then the client may have no case at all. For example, a judicial review case cannot be brought if a client cannot demonstrate that the body that carried out the act, omission or made the decision that is the subject of the dispute falls within the definition of a public body or a public authority. A problem question answer should address this issue early on, as if it cannot be proved, the client will have no case regardless of whether the other legal and factual issues can be proved. Take your lead from the general principles of law that govern the legal situation that is the subject of the problem.

Once you are sure that you have linked your ideas and that together they answer the question, then the final stage is to check your draft for spelling, grammar, footnotes and formatting issues.

7.1.2 GRAMMAR AND PUNCTUATION

Grammar worries most people a little bit and many of us a lot. It is one of the things that crops up time and time again in student feedback from assessments. Grammatical issues are not quite the same as stylistic ones – people adopt different styles of writing, but sentences do need to be grammatically correct, if they are to be understood. You are encouraged to adopt your own style of writing, within certain limits, but you do need to adhere to the basic rules of grammar. If you are unsure about punctuation issues you may wish to read *Eats, Shoots and Leaves*,[1] which is a humorous and practical guide to punctuation, which has also become a bestseller. If you are really worried about your English grammar then you may either decide to make use of a grammar book or to ask your personal tutor about English grammar and writing courses run by the university. Most universities do have very good 'writing for academic success' and 'English for academic purposes' courses for undergraduate and postgraduate students, and it may be as well to do the course towards the beginning of your degree, even if it means dropping a law option, rather than struggling with grammar issues throughout your studies. Apart from anything else, your grades will probably be much improved, if you undertake such a course. There are some basic rules that I shall mention here.

You must write in fully formed sentences, even if you are in a hurry and even if there is a much funkier way of writing the sentence in txt format. Surprising though it may sound, essays are occasionally submitted in which 'you' has become 'U' and 'to' has become '2'. Funny though this is, this style does not achieve good marks for a student in an assessment unless the marker has a particularly odd sense of humour. The bullet points below set out the mistakes frequently seen in law student written work, but for much greater assistance as regards Legal English do refer to Haigh's *Legal English* book, details of which are provided in the bibliography.

- Sentences must begin with a capital letter.
- Sentences must end with a full stop.
- Any words that are being quoted, where the words belong to someone else and not to the student, must be in quotation marks and must also

1 L. Truss, *Eats, Shoots and Leaves: The Zero Tolerance Approach to Punctuation* (Profile Books, 2003).

be referenced either through in-text references (Harvard style), end-notes or footnotes (usually conforming to the OSCOLA standard).

- Others' ideas (even if you have described them in your own words) must also be fully referenced too.
- Capital letters should only be used in the middle of a sentence for proper nouns or for abbreviations (assuming these have been defined earlier in the written work) or for other defined words.
- Check to see whether you are using a plural or a possessive or the possessive or an adverb or a possessive or a contraction. There are a couple of words that trip up some students:
  - 'It is' when shortened becomes 'it's' with an apostrophe. An apostrophe is not used for 'its' when it is used to explain that the thing in question belongs to 'it'. An example would be: *'Parliament has the power to self-regulate. Its power derives from parliamentary privilege.'* The same is true for who's – this denotes a contraction of 'who is' and the apostrophe signals the missing 'i', whereas the possessive is instead written as follows: *'whose case is this?'* Other possessive pronouns such as his, hers and theirs also do not include an apostrophe.
  - Plurals and possessives such as: *'the judges' voices were heard very clearly'* an example of plural (more than one judge) and possessive (the voices belonged to the judges so you need an apostrophe at the end to indicate the possessive); *'the judge's voice was heard very clearly'* is an example of a singular (one judge) and a possessive; *'the judges were heard very clearly'* is an example of a plural and no possessive.
  - Their, there and they're. Their is used to denote a possessive: *'The Mirror Group was involved in litigation with Naomi Campbell; their case involved issues of privacy and press freedom'* which could be expressed as *'the case that they were involved in'*. There is an adverb: *'Mirror Group Newspapers had to go to court; Campbell had to go there too'*. They're is a contraction and the apostrophe indicates a missing letter 'a' as the full phrase would be 'They are', similar to the contraction above of 'it's; short for 'it is': *'I expect that they're glad that it is all over.'*
- The colon (:) and semicolon (;) are often confused. A semicolon is used as a mini full stop to separate two clauses that are closely connected but not sufficiently distinctive so as to be two individual sentences. It should, however, be possible to read both as free-standing statements. A colon used before a list, for example: to allow you to separate different ideas; to allow you list a variety of factors. You'll

have seen that items in the list following the colon are often separated by a semicolon.

- Words such as Parliament, Government, the Judiciary are usually referred to in the singular rather than the plural and so 'the Government is considering' is more usual than 'the Government are', although there are differences of opinion on this.
- Check that you have not put down the wrong spelling of words that sound the same. Examples include: weather and whether; two, too and to.
- Words such as 'since' and 'while' can be difficult to use correctly. It is usually considered better practice to begin a sentence with 'Although it could be suggested that...' rather than 'Since' or 'While', although some people argue that this is a matter of style rather than grammar.
- Each new idea should be discussed in a new paragraph, and in a single paragraph. In other words do not start a new line for each new sentence.
- Spellcheck your work.

Many of us feel that we need more help with our grammar. Consider using a grammar book to assist you in your writing to begin with, and with luck you will find that your grammar gradually improves throughout your course. If you feel that you need extra help then ask your tutor whether there is a workshop or a module at your university that will help you to develop your writing skills.

 More resources are signposted via the companion website, including some web-based tests.

7.1.3 STYLE ISSUES

Style is a personal thing, and written style is no different. However, there are conventions about the style you should adopt in writing an essay or an answer to a problem question. The conventions include whether the writer should write in the active or passive voice and whether to refer to third parties as 'him' or 'her' or 'them'. Different types of written work require different styles of writing. This book has been written in a relatively informal style, making use of 'you' and 'I' to communicate skills techniques to you in what, I hope, is a clear way in the form of conversation. This style may also be appropriate for a reflective essay, in which you reflect on your skills development. Nonetheless, grammar and punctuation rules still apply. Most essays and problem question answers should adopt a style more similar to that seen in traditional textbooks, journal articles and cases. Formal written style is less personal and more distanced.

Problem questions are forms of professional writing, to a certain extent. They are a mode of communicating a professional opinion to another professional. These tend to be written without reference to *'you'* or *'I'*, but instead use phrases such as *'it is considered that...'* rather than *'I consider'* or *'I think'*. This adds authority to the opinion, as it makes the decision appear to be one that has been arrived at after professional deliberation. It gives it the aura of a professional rather than a personal decision. The more formal style provides extra gravity and distance and thus adds authority to it.

Essays and answers to problem questions are usually written in the passive voice. An example of the passive voice and the third person would be:

> *Parliamentary supremacy has been examined to establish whether supremacy has been eroded as a result of the UK's membership of the EU.*

An example of a similar sentence written in an active voice and in the first person would be:

> *I am considering whether the UK's membership of the EU has eroded Parliamentary supremacy.*

This second example shows two of the stylistic concerns that tutors may have with students' work. The more usual convention is that written assessments are written in the third person and the passive. There is no mention of *'I think'*, or *'My view is'*, or *'My opinion would be that'*. It may seem rather strange, but that is the way it is in most law schools. The assessment is personal to you in that you have done the research and the reading, made the notes, dissected the question, planned it and written an answer, but what you find and therefore what you write is supposed to be universal rather than personal – you are, rightly or wrongly, supposed to have hit upon the truth, or at least a truth, backed up by evidence, rather than simply a personal opinion. This is in keeping with traditional notions of professionalism (some would say these are very loaded notions that are based on a very particular masculine approach to professionalism and thus also to writing). You may be expected to remain distanced (and seemingly absent as an individual from the text) but you may also be expected to refer to authors by name in the text (for example *'Baxter indicates that...'*). Check with your tutor, if you are unsure or anxious about this. Some tutors may prefer you to write in the first person, particularly in the context of reflective or reflexive essays, journals or portfolios, in which case you should follow their instructions. This book breaks many of the conventions by writing directly to you, rather than writing to an impersonal audience, because it is trying to communicate directly with you. Most tutors will find it is more acceptable to write in an impersonal voice, to provide professional distance and add some weight to the writing. But some may actively encourage you to write in a more personal and conversational style.

7.1.4 FORMATTING AND PRESENTATION ISSUES

Most coursework will have to be word-processed and, if you are not sure how to use a computer, then it as well to take the opportunity of free computing lessons at university as soon as possible in your university career. It may feel comforting to put this off, but it will place you under more pressure at the point when you have to write your assessments.

Appropriate presentation is usually one of the assessment criteria against which your essay or problem question will be judged. Markers will obviously expect far more from you in presentation terms as regards coursework, when you have the time to work on formatting and presentation, than for work written under exam conditions, most of which will be handwritten. Check to see whether your course has standard requirements for word-processed answers. If not, then you may wish to make use of the following:

- Case names should be underlined if handwritten, or italicised or in bold, or underlined if typed.
- Quotation marks are usually single (' '), but may be double (" "). Some people use ' ' for the main quote and " " for quotes that come within the main quotes. However, the anti-plagiarism software Turnitin expects quotations to be enclosed with double marks (" ") and you may be asked to use these for all quotes so as to ensure that your work doesn't score a particularly high similarity index via that software.
- Quotations are usually kept within a paragraph unless they are three or four lines long, in which case they may be put on a new line and indented from the left.
- Numbers are usually written in words for number one to nine and then in figures from 10 onwards.
- Phrases such as 'for example' should normally be written in full in the main body of an essay, but may be abbreviated to 'e.g.' in footnotes.
- Abbreviated words such as *'don't'*, *'won't'*, *'shouldn't'* should normally be written in full as *'do not'*, *'will not'*, *'should not'*.
- Footnote numbers usually come at the end of sentences and after punctuation.[2] It is not that important, but do adopt a consistent approach whatever you decide to do.

---

2 Unless you need to refer to more than one footnote in a sentence, in which case you may put a footnote number in the middle of a sentence, or unless the footnote relates to one point in a sentence that contains more than one point.

- Headings should also be consistent. In other words, make sure that headings of the same level (subheading one, for example) look the same throughout your essay. Adopt a different style of heading for the next level of headings down.

Once you have checked the presentation and formatting issues, you are ready to move on to the final checking change.

7.2: FINAL CHECKS

- **Reread the question.**

- **Revisit any materials handed out with your assessment.**

- **Revisit any instructions you were given with the assessment including the word limit.**

- **Check the deadline date.**

- **Consider the assessment and grading criteria.**

- **Read through your essay one last time to check that it reads well, the references are complete and there are no typographical or spelling errors.**

Word limit – you are unlikely to achieve a good mark if you have written well under the word limit as the word limit indicates the level of detail and analysis that you need to include in your answer. Answers that are too brief usually lack sufficient research evidence to back up the points being made. It is as well to go back through the research stages to ensure that you have found as much relevant material as possible, and then interweave it into your answer. It should also assist in providing depth and authority to your answer. Answers that are well over the word limit may also be penalised. It may be that you can cut down your answer by some simple editing. Is it possible for you to simplify any of your sentences? Could you summarise some of your arguments or cut out irrelevant facts from case descriptions? Try to pare down your paragraphs to the essentials. Could you shorten sentences by removing lots of extra clauses and adding a few full stops? It is often possible to reduce the length of a passage by simply removing superfluous words (such as 'simply' in this sentence). Do you really need all those quotes, could you not paraphrase the important points instead? Check the word limit and the way it is calculated (are footnotes included in the limit for example?) with your lecturer.

Materials that have been handed out with the essay title – has your lecturer provided any other materials to which you may need to refer in order to answer the question fully? Have you taken these into account?

Assessment and grading criteria – check how you are being assessed. Chapter 1 provides some assistance on what assessment criteria mean as regards your writing.

Deadline date – Finally, make sure that you have handed in your work by the deadline. You may be penalised quite substantially if you fail to meet it. Many universities do not award a mark to work that has been handed in late, unless you are able to show extenuating or special circumstances. All your hard work may be wasted if you hand in your work late.

Next steps:

- **Reread your written work.**

- **Does it answer the question?**

- **Check how well it flows. Do your arguments link?**

- **How well does it read? Is the written English as it should be? Have you spellchecked your work?**

- **Does it meet the assessment guidelines in terms of format, length, etc.?**

- **You may want to test your understanding of stylistic issues by undertaking the brief task at the end of the chapter. The answers are towards the end of the book.**

- **If you remain concerned about your standard of written English and you do not think that referring to a grammar book is likely to solve the problem, then see your personal tutor to ask whether there are any courses designed for undergraduate students that you may take at the university.**

- **You may wish to review the examples of good and poor practice on the companion website.**

7.3: TEST YOUR UNDERSTANDING OF STYLE ISSUES

Rewrite the following sentences in an appropriate style for an essay:

1   *'I think that Parliamentary supremacy has been lost as a result of Britain joining the European Community.'*
2   *'The* Factortame *case played an important role in our understanding of the way in which European law must be interpreted by the courts. We now know that given a straight fight between British law and European law, European law will win.'*
3   *'We don't really know whether the Human Rights Act has been semi-entrenched within the British constitution, as no Parliament has yet attempted to repeal it. I think that Parliament would face a public outcry if it did try to repeal the Human Rights Act and so I believe that, in real terms, the Human Rights Act is really entrenched.'*

Read through a previous essay you have written. How does your writing style compare against the style you will adopt in future essays? What are the differences and how will your alter your written style in the future, if at all?

   You may want to test yourself further via the companion website.

SUMMARY

By finishing and polishing your written work, you hope to pick up on gaps in your arguments, poor use of expression, spelling and formatting errors and missing footnotes. This stage always takes longer than you think, so allow at least 24 hours to complete this stage before handing in work to be marked.

Once you have completed your essay in draft:

Leave it alone for 24 hours

Return to your essay

Overview check: read the draft to check it as a whole

Reread the question or problem and then reread your draft once through

Take note of the ideas and arguments in the draft. Start at the beginning and ask yourself the following questions:

'Have I answered the question?'
'Do I need to rearrange the order of ideas so that they flow?'
'Have I explained where my arguments are going throughout the essay?'
Have I grouped together ideas that point in one direction?'

Make any changes

Paragraph check: reread the draft again to check individual paragraphs

Read each paragraph and ask yourself the following questions:

'Have I stated the point I am making?'
'Have I explained my point?'
'Have I rounded off the point by explaining its relevance to the question?'
'Have I provided evidence to back up the point?'
Have I cited all my sources?'

Make any changes

Check your spellings and grammar

Final checks: reread your draft one final time

Check presentation and formatting

Check all citations are full and accurate. Check bibliography

8

LEGAL WRITING IN EXAMS AND HOW TO PREPARE

Legal writing in exams is very similar to legal writing in coursework essays and problem-based coursework. Students still need to follow similar steps in the writing process; however, the nature of the exam will change the marker's expectations of a written answer. This chapter will take you through the different types of law exams and the way this will affect your essay and problem question answers.

8.1: TYPES OF LAW EXAMS

- **Unseen exams:** you do not see the paper or have knowledge of the questions in advance.

- **Seen exams:** you are given the paper/questions in advance to prepare.

- **Closed-book exams:** you may not take materials into the exams.

- **Open-book exams:** you may take specified materials into the exams.

The majority of law exams are unseen exams, which means that you will not have the questions in advance. Seen exams are exams for which you have either been given some or all of the questions or the exam paper itself in advance. There are two other main permutations as well, which are that the exam will be a closed-book one, meaning that you will not be permitted to take any materials into the exam with you, or open-book, in which you will be permitted to take in some materials and to refer to them. You need to be clear on the type of exam you will be sitting and prepare accordingly as they assess your knowledge, skills and qualities differently.

8.2: TYPES OF QUESTIONS

- Multiple choice: you are set a series of questions and have a choice of answers for each question. You select the most appropriate one (or other as stated on the paper).

- Short-answer questions: you are set questions that require you to answer it in only a few sentences and in no more than a paragraph.

- Essay-based questions: you are given a title or a question and then asked to answer it in an essay format.

- Problem questions: you are given a factual scenario and you are asked to advise a client or clients on their legal position.

The paper may contain four main different types of questions: multiple-choice questions, short-answer questions, essay-based questions and problem questions. Multiple-choice questions do not require a written answer, but the other three types of questions require an answer written in full sentences with evidence to back up the points that are being made. Essays and problem questions should also be written using proper paragraphs. Short-answer questions test particular discrete elements of knowledge, whereas essays and problems questions test a wider range of knowledge. The legal writing steps remain the same for different types of exams, but your preparation for them should be a little different.

8.3: DIFFERENT TECHNIQUES

You should adopt a different technique and type of preparation for different types of exam and different types of questions.

You need to develop different sets of skills to perform well.

But there are some similarities as well.

The keys to success are:

- preparation;

- know your paper;

- sort out your timing;

- spend time reading the paper.

Your preparation should always involve you looking through past exam papers for each exam you will sit. It is extremely important that you know whether your paper is to be seen or unseen, whether it will be open-book (and if so what materials you will be permitted) or closed-book. It is also important that you know the anatomy of the paper, for example the number of questions on the paper in comparison with the number you have to answer. You should also check whether you must answer particular questions or whether you have a completely free choice of questions on the paper. You should be clear on the length of time you have to write each answer, by dividing the total writing time available to you (this may be the same as the exam length, or slightly less if there is compulsory reading time as part of the exam) by the number of questions you must answer, assuming all questions are worth the same number of marks. That way, you narrow down the number of possible surprises during the exam. Most LLB or graduate diploma papers are relatively standard from year to year and thus it should be possible to be very well prepared before you enter the exam room.

Once you have entered the exam you should check that you have the correct paper in front of you and you should read the instructions on the front cover very carefully. A number of students fail exams unnecessarily each year, because they have not followed the instructions correctly and have answered too few or too many questions on the paper, or they have not answered a compulsory question. Once the exam starts, read through each question on the paper first, then return to the questions that you think you may answer and focus on those. But, before you get too focused on the paper, ensure that you are clear on how long you have to answer each question, and if you are prone to getting carried away and spending too long on a question then write down the time at which you will need to move on to the next question, and the next. It is very rare that you will make up enough marks in an answer that you wrote well over the time allocation, to counterbalance a very short or panicked answer at the end when you were running out of time. Consistency is the key, as is being aware of the time and being able to see a clock. Many students arrive without a watch, are surprised when they are told they cannot use their mobile phone as a clock (it is a communication device – of course you cannot use it!) – and then find they cannot quite make out the numbers on the clock at the front of the exam room. Please be prepared.

This may be the appropriate point to say a few things about nerves and performance. Many of us will find that we perform at our best when under a little bit of pressure, but when it tips over into too much we start to make silly mistakes at best, and become paralysed by fear at worst. You are not alone if you find law exams a very daunting prospect. For many of us, and at most times in our lives, were are able to calm ourselves down by getting a good night's sleep, eating well, not drinking too many caffeinated drinks, talking through our anxiety with someone we trust and doing a sensible amount of preparation in advance of the examination period. You may find it helpful to draw up a realistic revision timetable to begin about four weeks ahead of the examination period. Be sure to mark in break times and time off as well as putting down a structured and realistic approach to revision given the schedule of the forthcoming exams. Although it is difficult to make up for a lack of work during the academic year by a hefty dose of revision just before the exams, it is certainly possible to improve your marks during this period. However, the pressure can get too much at times and it is important to recognise the signs. If you feel that you are becoming really anxious about the prospect of exams then please see your personal tutor, academic advisor or student mentor to get some guidance. That will often be enough to get you back on track, but if not then they will most likely to able to direct you to other sources of support and guidance.

8.4: SIMILARITIES FOR ALL ESSAY AND PROBLEM QUESTION ANSWERS

> Dissect the question you have selected. Read it and then read it again. Many marks get wasted because students misread the questions or instructions.
>
> Plan your answer. Do not start writing straight away without planning.
>
> Check through your answers at the end if you have time, while checking the questions and instructions again.

You should approach your essay or problem question answer in the same way as you would outside an exam room, although you will be writing under timed exam conditions and consequently you will not have time to nip to the library to do any research, nor to write for as long as you would normally write for a piece of coursework. This actually makes your task much easier, rather than more challenging, believe it or not. If you have revised the topic that is the subject of the question and prepared for possible questions in advance, the writing process should be very straightforward. You should simply need to dissect the question and then jot down all the issues that you think may be relevant to answering it. Then note down any points that you need to make as regards each issue, put down any evidence to which you need to refer and consider how the issue relates to the question. Reread the question to make sure you are clear on your task, then begin writing. Follow the structure of the essay as set out below, if you are in any doubt about how to write an essay.

8.5: STRUCTURING AN ESSAY ANSWER

- Make a list of relevant issues.

- Briefly jot down any evidence that relates to each issue.

- Organise your ideas into a logical order.

- Start writing.

Structuring an essay answer:

- Start with an introduction.

- Explain what the question is asking you to write about and which issues you will consider in order to answer it.

Middle section of the essay:

- Organise your ideas into paragraphs, one idea per paragraph.

- Start your paragraph by introducing the idea to the reader.

- Develop and discuss the issue, back up what you are saying about the issue with evidence.

- Conclude the paragraph by explaining how or why the issue is relevant to the question.

Conclusion:

- Pull the issues together in the conclusion to come to a final answer to the question.

- Do not go back through all the evidence.

- Do not introduce new ideas.

As you will see, the structure of an essay answer is very similar to the structure we developed in Chapter 2. This means setting up your revision notes in such a way as to allow you to know the key issues for each topic, the evidence that you would use to back up your discussion of each issue and the relevance of each issue to the topic. You may wish to follow the revision guide on the companion website to help with this, or you may wish to draw mind maps, flow-charts or diagrams that allow you to see the structure of each topic along with the authoritative evidence too.

8.6: STRUCTURING A PROBLEM QUESTION ANSWER

Important: Who are you advising? All the parties or named individuals?

Remember that a good lawyer does not give a one-sided viewpoint.

Start off each paragraph by making the point rather than by pointing out the evidence for a point you have not yet made.

Therefore, do not start a paragraph with a discussion of the facts of a case. Cases are evidence of the law as stated in legislation or the common law. Make your point first, then use the case(s) to back it up.

Remember to advise your client; do not just talk about the general legal position.

Problem question answers are not that different in structure, although the arguments you are advancing are a little different. Follow the structure for essay writing, but bear the following points in mind as you do so.

A good lawyer does not give a one-sided legal opinion at this stage of a case. It is dangerous to ignore the possible legal pitfalls that the client may experience if the case were to come to court. You should be realistic about your client's chances. If there is case law that weakens your client's case then say so as well as providing case law that supports it. Angle your question towards your client's situation rather than writing an opinion on how the law stands on the legal topic that is the subject of the problem. You will not do well if you answer a problem question by providing an essay on the law of judicial review, for example. Instead, you should refer to your client's case in each paragraph and you should use cases and statutory references to back up the points you make, but not as a way of discussing the law in general terms.

You must provide evidence to back up your points in problem questions and this evidence is evidence that could be cited in court. Cases that have precedent value are extremely important. The judgments from other courts in England and Wales that may not have a binding precedent authority may also be persuasive if they address the same point(s) of law as your client's case. The judgments of Commonwealth jurisdictions may also be persuasive in the same way as non-precedent cases above. No other sources are classed as 'legal sources'. Occasionally, academic texts are referred to as evidence of the law if there is no case law on the point or if the case law is terribly confused. Certain sections of *Hansard* may be referred to as an aid to the interpretation of legislation by judges.

8.7: REVISION TECHNIQUES

- You need to revise for an exam not for a subject.

- In other words, you must look at the past papers before you start your revision so that you are clear on the type and range of questions and the time you will have to answer them.

- Learning chunks of information will not get you a high mark for essay and problem questions, but may for multiple-choice exams.

- You need to be clear on the general principles for each topic that could be the subject of a question you will answer.

- You should revise by considering what the general principles of law are for a given topic.

- You then need to work out what evidence you have to back them up from cases, legislation and from academic opinion where the cases or legislation are not clear-cut.

- You need to be clear on how the topics fit together in the subject.

There is little point in learning large chunks of information unless you are about to sit a multiple-choice exam. Essay and problem questions are set to test your understanding of the law and to make sure that you know the general principles of each topic on which you are examined. But they are also designed to test how well you can use your knowledge to answer the specifics of a question, and this is key. They are not a way to test how much law you can remember from your lectures. You should prepare for these types of essays by revising the general principles for each topic, as well as the evidence that supports the principles. You should also practise dissecting questions and working out which issues are relevant to them.

One of the easiest ways to revise for unseen exams involving problems questions and essay questions is as follows. Take a piece of paper and write the topic that you are revising at the top. The topics will have been set out in the module handbook or the lecture schedule. Next, read through your lecture notes, your textbook and other notes and make a list of issues that crop up within that topic. These are the general principles of the topic. Your list will look similar to the ones you have made at the planning stage of your essays and problem questions, although they will be more extensive. Write a sentence or a couple of sentences under each of the issues that are on your list, which explain the nature of the general principle. Add in the detail of the principle and add in any evidence that you have to back up these points. Again, this is similar to an essay plan or a problem question plan, but is much more detailed. You should now have notes on a topic on two sides of A4, including a list of topics (which are the general principles) with a brief explanation of each, followed by sub-issues for each topic and evidence to back them up. If you do not understand any aspect of the information you have on your sheet of paper then you should go back to your notes and reread that section. You will not be able to write a good essay if you do not understand the issues. Finally, you need to learn the information on the sheet.

 Visit the companion website at www.routledge.com/cw/webley for an example of a revision sheet.

Once in the exam you will identify those questions that you will answer. After dissecting the question you can simply note down the general principles in a plan, one per paragraph and jot down the supporting information you can remember from your sheet of paper. Some of the principles from the sheet will not be relevant and those can be crossed out; some you may not remember; however, you will already have a basic essay or problem question plan prepared prior to the exam, which should take the pressure off you.

 Visit the companion website at www.routledge.com/cw/webley for an example of how to convert your revision into a good quality written answer.

8.8: PREPARATION FOR OPEN-BOOK EXAMS

> **If you are allowed to take a notebook or folder in with you:**
>
> - Make sure you know the regulations for the notebook; for example, must it contain handwritten notes, be a certain size, etc.?
>
> - Include as much *useful* material on the topic as possible including evidence to back up the points. This sometimes means taking in less material that the maximum amount permitted.
>
> - Make sure you understand the information that is in there. The exam is not the best place to try to make sense of the topic.
>
> - Organise the book so that you know where to find things as quickly as possible.
>
> - Check whether you are permitted to highlight or underline materials.

Lecturers will expect more from your answer if you have access to information in a notebook, a statute book or a textbook in the exam. This means your answer should include more evidence to back up your points, as you will have access to that evidence rather than having to remember it as you would in a closed-book exam. There will be an expectation that you will have the general principles at your fingertips, plus cases and statutes and academic quotes.

You will need to spend time preparing your materials for the exam. Make sure that you know whether you are permitted to underline or highlight passages, or to write in books that can be taken in. If you get this wrong then, at best, your materials will be taken from you. There is little point having material with you that you cannot use in the exam. The more time you spend flicking through your books, the less time you have to write. Less generally means more in terms of notes or materials. It is better that you have fewer notes that are focused and which you can use, than that you arrive with three folders of material that you do not know at all. Index your materials if you are allowed to do so, and make sure that you have full citations for any sources that you will draw upon. The plagiarism rules will apply to any work that you cite from your notebook, so be sure to cite your sources.

8.9: MOST FREQUENT REASONS FOR FAILURE IN EXAMS

- Did not answer the correct number of questions having misunderstood the instructions;

- Ran out of time and did not answer the correct number of questions;

- Did not answer the question set/misunderstood the question and answered one they made up themselves;

- Wrote an essay on the general law rather than advising the client in a problem question;

- Had not looked at past papers before the exam and so did not know what to expect.

Sadly we do not always do as well as we would hope in exams, and it is worth remembering that an exam is a test of knowledge on a particular day, not an assessment of the effort that you have put in during the course of the year or your level of intelligence. Sometimes students fail exams because they do not know anything about the subject upon which they are being examined. More usually they fail because they have not demonstrated their knowledge and skills in the right way by answering the correct number of questions set within the given time period. Many of these kinds of mistakes are avoidable if a student has prepared for an exam and has read the instructions properly before they start.

Finally, the main theme of this chapter is preparation. It is relatively easy to do well if you know the types of question you will be asked, the time you have to write each answer and, if you have revised the general principles, the evidence that backs them up and the way in which the general principles fit together. It is hard to do well if you enter the exam room unsure of what you have to do or how you will be tested. Prepare well and hopefully you will do well too. If, however, you find that you have not achieved the mark you expected, or you would hope for, ask for feedback from your tutor once you have your results. There are usually things one can learn that will improve your marks for the future and there are very, very few students who cannot get through law exams with reasonable marks, because if we had doubts about your ability we probably would not have given you a place on the course in the first instance. Ask for feedback and use it as a way to improve your marks in the future. The next chapter provides some guidance on frequent feedback given to students to assist them to improve their performance.

Next steps:

- Read through the information in your module/course handbooks to check how you will be assessed in each module/course.

- Make sure that you attend all revision lectures and tutorials and that you do any preparation that is required of you. These sessions are usually designed to give you useful feedback that will help your exam preparation.

- Look through past papers for each module/course. Check how many questions you have to answer, of what type, how much choice you get and how long you have to answer each question.

- Read through the assessment and grading criteria, if you can get hold of copies; if not, then refresh your memory of the generic grading criteria by rereading Chapter 1.

Now begin your exam revision, in the light of your understanding of how you will be assessed.

 You may wish to look at the additional resources on the companion website to help with your legal writing technique in exams.

SUMMARY

The basic rules of revision technique are as follows:

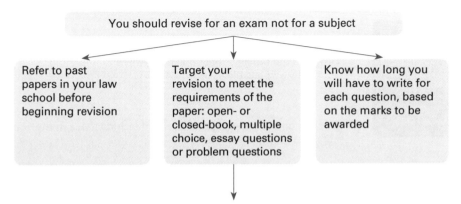

You should revise for an exam not for a subject

| Refer to past papers in your law school before beginning revision | Target your revision to meet the requirements of the paper: open- or closed-book, multiple choice, essay questions or problem questions | Know how long you will have to write for each question, based on the marks to be awarded |

Begin revision

Target revision at the topics that have been covered in detail in lectures and tutorials, unless you have been told otherwise

You may wish to spend more time revising topics that occur frequently in past exam papers, although do so with care as syllabi do change from year to year

Multiple choice exams → Learn the detail from lecture, tutorial and textbook notes

Essay questions and problem questions

Closed-book exams

Be clear on the general principles for each topic from lecture, tutorial and textbook notes. Learn the general principles

Learn evidence in support of the general principles, including the ratio, not just the facts of the case

Learn any evidence that limits the general principles, or adds exceptions to those principles

Essay questions and problem questions

Open-book exams

Be clear on the regulations relating to the materials that can be taken into the exam

Include as much useful material as possible on the possible topics, including evidence to back up the points

Organise the book so that you know where to find things as quickly as possible

Be clear on the general principles and include those in the notebook

Include evidence in respect of the general principles

Once in the exam:

Check you have the correct paper

↓

Read the instructions carefully to check how many questions you have to answer, whether there are compulsory questions, the time you have to write, etc.

↓

Read all the questions. Read them again and select those you are able to answer. Note down the times when you need to move on to your next answer

↓

Take each question you will answer in turn as follows:

• Make a list of relevant issues
• Briefly jot down any evidence that relates to each issue
• Organise your ideas into a logical order
• Start writing your answer

↓

Follow the essay-writing and problem answer guides in Chapters 2 and 3, ensure you have evidence to back up each point made

↓

Take each question in turn. Do not spend longer on one question at the detriment of another

↓

Check your work, if you have time

9

USING FEEDBACK TO IMPROVE PERFORMANCE

Lecturers find themselves writing similar comments on many of the essays and problem question answers they mark. It is not that they are churning out the same old comments, or at least that is generally not the case, but that the same issues keep cropping up in students' work. This book has attempted to show you how to make the most of your legal writing to achieve the highest possible marks, but if you find that you are receiving comments on the need to improve your essay structure, your focus in answering the question, your references and citations, your use of bibliographies and your use of grammar, then the comments below may assist a little. Some of these explanations have been expanded upon in previous chapters. To make the most of your (admittedly limited) feedback opportunities, it is suggested that you do the following in conjunction with the feedback you have received:

1 Reread the assessment question and guidelines.

2 Reread the assessment and grading criteria.

3 Reread your assessed piece of work. How would you grade it? Why? What could you have done to improve?

4 Reread your feedback. How does that compare with your assessment of your written work? Do you need to talk to your tutor, or do you understand why you have received the mark and the comments that you have received?

5 Look back at your written work again. What relatively minor changes could have improved your work a good deal? What other modifications would take much more work?

6 What does this tell you about how you should approach future written work? How will you ensure that you build on your performance this time, so that you improve?

Reflection on one's performance is an integral part of the learning cycle and we miss out on good learning opportunities if we give feedback only a cursory glance and then consign it to a folder or a drawer. There are relatively few opportunities for feedback on written work, so it is as well to make the most of those that are available. The next sections try to decode some of the feedback that you may see on your work.

9.1: COMMON FEEDBACK ON IMPROVING ESSAY STRUCTURE

- Your written work should begin with an introduction that explains how you will approach the question.

- Your essay should be divided into paragraphs made up of sentences. Each paragraph should contain one main idea or issue. Paragraphs should follow on from each other and should be organised into an order that allows the ideas to develop into arguments. State the issue to be discussed at the beginning of each paragraph.

- A paragraph should begin with a sentence that sets out the idea or issue to be discussed within it. The middle section of the paragraph should discuss the issue and provide evidence in support of the discussion. Others' work should be referenced in footnotes or endnotes. The paragraph should then conclude by explaining the relevance of the issues to the question by stating what it means or why it is important as regards the question.

- Your essay should end with a conclusion that draws together the issues discussed in each paragraph, but which does not explain the detail of those issues. It should summarise them and provide a final answer to the question.

All of these comments are about communicating ideas effectively to the reader. A well-structured essay allows the reader to follow the arguments put forward and to weigh up the evidence. A poorly structured essay may detract from the arguments, confuse the reader and appear to deviate from the question. A well-structured essay may contain the same content as the poorly constructed essay and yet the marks awarded would be very different. Communication is an important skill, and the structure of an essay will determine how well the ideas are communicated.

9.2: COMMON FEEDBACK ABOUT IMPROVING FOCUS TO ANSWER TO THE QUESTION

- You are marked on your ability to answer the question that has been set. You are not marked on your general understanding of the subject or the topic.

- You should spend some time analysing and dissecting the question to be sure that you understand the task that has been set. You may wish to rewrite the question in your own words or to make a list of the issues encompassed by the question.

- You should research the topics that are the subject of the question, by reading through your lecture and textbook notes and working out important themes. Then plan your research and your writing in the light of the question. Reread the question regularly to make sure that you are specifically addressing it.

- Make sure that you explain in your answer why and how each point you make is relevant to the question. If you cannot make a point relevant then do not include it.

This feedback relates to the student's ability to diagnose the problem set, or to dissect the question asked. The essay may be well structured, clearly written, well evidenced and presented, and correctly referenced, but if it does not answer the question the mark awarded will be towards the lower end of the spectrum. Similar issues arise in problem answers when students have not spent enough time working through the facts, sorting out which are agreed and which may not be agreed, as well as what information is missing that may be needed. Students who have received this kind of feedback should spend longer on the diagnosis stage, by splitting up the question into the main topic and then the issues to be discussed, or dissecting the problem question into constituent facts, prior to researching the relevant law.

9.3: COMMON FEEDBACK ON ANALYSIS AND EVIDENCE

- The answer is very descriptive or is insufficiently analytical. There is a lack of evidence in support of the points being made. The essay needs to be more critical.

- Strong analysis is a product of being clear on the question, undertaking good quality research (or having done good quality preparation for tutorials that has led on to high-quality revision notes for closed-book exams), organising one's ideas into themes and working from there to construct strong paragraphs that are well linked to allow for high-level analysis to be developed.

- You develop analysis by first describing an idea that you have read/seen/heard as succinctly as possible. Then you consider what that idea means in the context of the question, how it helps to answer the question and note that down too (the start of analysis). Then you redraft and redraft again so as to write out the description and write in the analysis.

- All the material on a single theme or idea should be grouped together to allow you to read through all that material and work out what is your conclusion. That goes to the beginning of the paragraph.

- You then redraft the middle section of your paragraph so that it becomes the justification or explanation as to how you reached that conclusion. Each sentence is redrafted so that your analysis (point) comes first and your evidence then follows. You should try to have multiple sources of authoritative evidence for each point, and it must be a full spectrum of views and not just the sources that agree with our personal views.

- You reread the question, then your paragraph and consider what is your new, higher level conclusion, then add that at the end of the paragraph.

- You repeat these stages for each paragraph and between paragraphs so as to maximise your chances of developing analysis that builds on what you have learned in other paragraphs. You continue to redraft until you have nothing more to add.

- Your final draft should read as if you knew the answer all along, in other words you need to redraft your essay so that it reflects the state of your knowledge at the end of the process.

Most of us will receive feedback that our work is too descriptive, insufficiently analytical and/or lacks authority or evidence. It is all part of the learning journey. Basically the feedback indicates one of three things: insufficient research and reading which means that you have very little to draw upon to develop your analysis, your conclusions; insufficient consideration of how the material in each paragraph helps you to answer the question – you have skipped on to the next issue without asking yourself the 'so what?' question; and/or insufficient redrafting of each paragraph so as to develop your analysis into critical analysis and to disperse your analysis through the whole paragraph and each sentence. In many instances all three issues will be present. For future assessment be sure to plan and conduct your research so as to maximise the range of authoritative sources you find and have the time to read. You may want to revisit your note-taking technique in case you are not capturing the material that will help you to come to conclusions about the question. The other issues are largely ones of redrafting and reflecting, which can be remedied by following the steps outlined in earlier chapters. As long as you have sufficient time to redraft, reflect on what you have found and what it means in the light of the question, redraft again and repeat, you should be well on your way to critical analysis. But if not, or you think that you would benefit from some extra help, seek help from your tutor.

9.4: COMMON FEEDBACK ON CITATION/ REFERENCES AND BIBLIOGRAPHIES

- You must cite all the sources that you have referred to in your essay. This includes any words you have used from others' works or any ideas that you came across in others' works.

- You should cite sources in either footnotes or endnotes and you should retain a consistent style throughout your work.

- The reader should be able to look up each of the quotations or ideas you have referred to by taking the reference you have cited and using it to find them. Citations must be full and accurate.

- If you refer to a source and find that you need to refer to the source that your source has cited, then you must cite both sources: your source (which will be the secondary source) and their source (the primary source).

- A bibliography should contain all the sources that you have drawn upon in the process of your writing. This will include all of your own sources that you cited in your footnotes (not primary sources from your secondary sources, however) as well as other works that shape your ideas but which you have not directly cited in your footnotes/endnotes.

- A bibliography should be arranged in alphabetical order, usually by the authors' last names.

- You should group books under one heading, cases under another, etc., according to the range of sources to which you have referred. A good bibliography will include a range of sources.

- You should cite your sources in full.

The feedback is specific and relatively easy to put into practice in subsequent essays. Be sure that when you take notes you summarise others' ideas in your own words or quote properly and enclose the quote in quotation marks. Keep a full and accurate record of all sources to which you have referred in your research phase (including exact page references) and follow the referencing conventions set out in Chapter 6. Proofread the essay or problem question answer before submitting it for assessment, to check that all footnotes are complete.

9.5: COMMON FEEDBACK ON SPELLING, PUNCTUATION, GRAMMAR AND STYLE

- You should check your written work to make sure that you have eliminated spelling errors and editing errors, as far as possible.

- You should read your work through to make sure that the sentences make sense.

- You are being assessed, in part, on your ability to communicate your ideas effectively, and poor grammar and poor spelling will detract from the ideas that you are trying to communicate. Most universities provide assistance with written English, so if you are concerned about your grammar then do talk to your personal tutor to find out what assistance is available within the university.

- Avoid using phrases that may be appropriate in everyday speech but that are not appropriate in written work, including slang, for example *'Dicey was like interested in the role of Parliament'.*

- Pay special attention to words that end in an 's', as these words may be plurals or they may be words that indicate that something belongs to someone or to something, for example: *'The students in the library'* (plural as there was more than one student in the library); *'The student's books were in the library'* (one student had left her books in the library and the apostrophe indicates that the books in the sentence belonged to the student).

- It is important that you check your work thoroughly before submitting it for assessment, as many errors are avoidable.

Most spelling errors are easy to correct using a spellcheck facility on the computer, assuming that the default language has been set correctly to 'English (United Kingdom)' rather than to 'English (United States)', for example. Many word-processing packages also have a grammar check facility, although these can sometimes be misleading, and consequently should be used with care.

The sections above give you a range of frequent feedback and advice, but you may not be able to decode the mark that you have been awarded. Chapter 1 focused on assessment and grading criteria and provided an analysis of what marks within different classifications mean in relation to student performance. Read through these again, if you are in doubt about what the mark you have been awarded means in respect of your own performance in an essay or problem question answer. A student who has been awarded a mark under 40% (assuming that 40% is the pass mark) needs to spend more time dissecting the question and getting to grips with the tasks. Once clear on the question, s/he should spend time reading through lecture and tutorial notes before carrying out research on the question. This should be translated into a plan and then into the essay, following the steps described in previous chapters. A student who has been awarded a mark of 40–49% has probably written an answer on the topic that is the subject of the question, but not on the question itself. A student who has been awarded a mark of 50–59% should concentrate on identifying the issues relevant to the question and using his or her research findings to construct an argument to answer the question. A student who has been awarded a mark of 60–69%, and who wishes to improve, should concentrate on developing his or her analysis of each issue by adding a sentence at the end of each paragraph, stating why and how the issue is relevant to the question, as well as undertaking further reading to provide depth to arguments within essays. A student who has been awarded a mark of 70% or more has done extremely well indeed; however, a student achieving first-class marks should still review his or her performance, as there are always lessons to be learned. Plus, it is not always easy to replicate excellent marks in all subjects and so generic lessons are useful to transfer to other modules/courses and forms of assessment.

Writing technique tends to improve with practice. In addition, it also helps to read through the feedback from previous essays and then to refer to the question and the assessment criteria again to see whether you can learn from previous experience. It is also a good idea to reread your essay once you have received your mark and feedback, even though this can be a painful exercise. However, it is often possible to be able to see where one could improve, if the essay is reread along with the feedback. This is the best way to ensure that essay writing technique, and marks, improve in the future. But do see your personal tutor or subject tutor if you remain unsure of what you need to do to improve after reading through your work and your feedback.

9.6: REFLECTION AND PERSONAL DEVELOPMENT PLANNING

Many law students will be asked to keep a learning log, journal or contribute to a personal development plan as part of their studies, and reflection on your performance in written assessment it can be a very powerful and positive way to learn. We learn through experience and by reflecting on those experiences.

You may reflect on your assessment experience including:

- how did you approach the assessment?

- what went well and why?

- what did not go as well and why?

- how did you feel about the assessment and the feedback, how do you feel now?

- what have you learned as a result of the experience?

- of what do you remain unsure and how will you seek clarity?

- what will you do differently next time?

- what additional steps do you need to take to ensure that you build on this experience, when will you take them, what support do you need to take them?

Although something of a generalisation, it is usual to find that students who improve their performance with each successive assessment, and those who receive consistently high marks, are students who actively reflect on their performance drawing upon the feedback they have received. All too often the students who are frequently surprised and disappointed by their marks are the ones who focus on the mark, only give a cursory reading to the feedback (some do not even access it or pick it up), blame others for their performance (the lack of books, the lack of time, the poor lecturer, their tutor…) and so go on to repeat the same patterns of poor practice again and again. That is not to say that extrinsic factors do not affect performance, but if some students in a year-group achieve very high marks, others middling, yet others low marks, then those differences are largely attributable to the individuals rather than the anything structural.

The good news is that honest, self-critical but constructive reflection on one's performance tends to yield positive improvements, just as it helps to move from description to analysis to critical analysis. And so it is well worth reading through any feedback you receive, read through your assessment again too, then consider the questions above by way of a self-appraisal of performance. Try to avoid being negative although I know that can be difficult if you are really disappointed with your performance. Your learning log is an opportunity to put a positive plan in place ahead of your next assessment, with support from others such as your tutor. Do talk to your tutor if you would like further feedback or help with next steps. Writing is a learning journey – with each new piece you write you have the opportunity to reflect on past performance and to improve.

Next steps:

- Follow the steps at the beginning of this chapter for each piece of written work that you have had marked.

- Then consider feedback that you have received on previous written work. Do any common themes emerge?

- What do you need to do to improve your written work? How will you put this into practice? Do you need any further assistance from a tutor?

SUMMARY

Feedback provided by the marker is intended to help you to understand why you were awarded the mark given for the assessment. However, it is also a tool to assist you in improving your written work in the future – known as feedforward. You should try to learn as much as you can from your previous performance, and use this to develop your approach, research, structure and written style in subsequent essays.

Before you undertake a piece of written work, look at previous feedback to remind yourself of potential pitfalls and how to avoid them in this work.

Once you have received feedback on your current essay, consider the following:

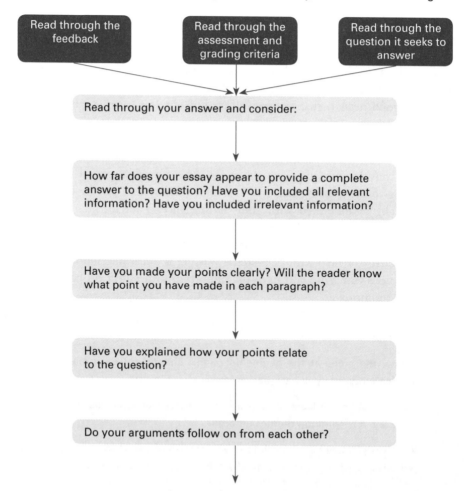

Read through the feedback

Read through the assessment and grading criteria

Read through the question it seeks to answer

Read through your answer and consider:

How far does your essay appear to provide a complete answer to the question? Have you included all relevant information? Have you included irrelevant information?

Have you made your points clearly? Will the reader know what point you have made in each paragraph?

Have you explained how your points relate to the question?

Do your arguments follow on from each other?

Have you provided authoritative evidence to back
up all your assertions?

Have you provided full citations to all quotes and all ideas
you have employed from others' work?

Reread the feedback. Does this accord with your views
of your essay? If you are still unsure about what you
could improve in the future, see your tutor to discuss it
with him or her

Consider what you will do differently in future essays and
problem question answers to improve your marks in
subsequent written work

Seek help from your subject tutor or personal tutor if you
remain unsure about the feedback or what you need to do
to improve

ANSWERS TO QUESTIONS

CHAPTER 1: APPLY YOUR KNOWLEDGE OF ASSESSMENT CRITERIA

'The British Parliament was once supreme.' Discuss with reference to Britain's membership of the EU and its obligations in relation to the European Convention on Human Rights.

Identifies the main topic in issue in the question, which is good

The sentence style needs a little work, and it is not usual to provide evidence or examples in the introduction. There was an attempt to outline the relevant issues to be discussed

This issue of parliamentary sovereignty has been that Parliament has been sovereign throughout centuries until the UK joined the European Community (European Communities Act 1972). Theorists such as Dicey have argued that Parliament is so power-ful and so totally sovereign that it is allowed to do anything that it wishes, even to order that smoking on the streets of Paris could be outlawed by the UK Parliament. However, there are those who disagree with this and the essay will consider opinions for and against whether Parliament is supreme or not.

Demonstrates that there are differing views and these will be considered, also good

An attempt to set out the main topic and some of the issues that will be discussed in the essay. The introduction would have been even more powerful, if it had also signposted membership of the Council of Europe, and left the evidence on supremacy until the main body of the essay

This sentence does introduce, in relatively simplistic terms, the argument to be advanced. This is a good start, but there are ways of introducing the point in a more subtle way

This is a very general and forceful statement, without any evidence in support

Correct to an extent, although it may be helpful to note that the ECA 1972 is a British Act of Parliament, just as the writer states in a later paragraph in respect of the HRA 1998

It may be considered that sovereignty has been lost from Parliament. This is because Britain joined Europe and Europe's power overtook the power of the British Parliament. This was done through the enactment of the ECA 1972. Many are of the belief that the Act is now entrenched, that Parliament cannot repeal it. There was a recent case about this where a man wanted to weigh his fruit and vegetables in pounds and was told he could not because Europe says that we must all use kilogrammes and grammes. This shows that Parliament is no longer supreme.

Again, a general and forceful statement with no evidence in support. Who says so?
Is their view authoritative and what is it based on?

The conclusion fits with what the student has said in the paragraph, which is good, but is not sufficiently nuanced given a proper reading of the evidence that s/he was trying to present

The student should have read the case – *Thoburn* – and if s/he had done this, the point would likely have been made more clearly. In addition, the ratio does not evidence the point being made

A good attempt at a fully developed paragraph, but the student does not appear to have read the evidence to which s/he refers and this pulls down the marks. The student also makes some sweeping statements without evidence to back them up

It would have been better to begin the paragraph without the use of the word 'however'. 'However' tends to be used within a paragraph, but not at the beginning of a new paragraph. It may have been better to say something along the lines of 'There are commentators who consider, in contrast, that Parliament remains supreme even given membership of the EU'.

However, there is a dispute about this point. The case of British Railways Board v. Pickin demonstrates that no Act of Parliament can be held to be invalid. This suggests that the courts must apply a British Act of Parliament and that Parliament can enact any law that it wishes; as long as the Act is passed it will become law in this country.

This case is relevant evidence, but it would have been better to begin the sentence with the point being made, followed by the evidence in support. In addition, the evidence needed to be used in more detail, to illustrate the point, as a case name does not convey the legal principle that the case established in this regard. The marker may wonder whether the student has read the case.

A reasonably good conclusion to the point being made. However, given the lack of detail in the sentence that preceded it, it is difficult for the reader to know whether it is accurate or not.

With a little more work, this could have been a good paragraph, assuming that more detail was provided and sources were cited fully and accurately.

Useful evidence but the student needed to introduce the point to be discussed. It may have been better to add this sentence onto the paragraph above to allow the argument to be developed properly. The facts of the case are oversimplified and therefore not entirely correct. It would also have been better to explain the *ratio* of *Factortame (No. 2)* – the appropriate case – and then the importance of the *ratio* as regards the essay question

*However, the **Factortame** case in the 1990s shows another side to this situation as the British courts did not apply the British Act of Parliament – the Merchant Shipping Act – but they applied the European law instead as they had been told they must by the European Court of Justice.*

This is not really a full paragraph. The student should have developed a whole idea fully in a paragraph, and provided evidence in support of the idea, as well as a conclusion to the point being made. Also, it would have been better to avoid using the word 'however' after using it previously. Perhaps instead 'There are cases that appear to contradict this assessment, however . . .' would have been more appropriate

Not accurate. Parliament may legislate contrary to the ECHR, even though it would be a breach of the ECHR and the UK could be sanctioned by the ECtHR in international law. Consequently the conclusion that flows from that sentence is not correct. The student has confused the terms of the HRA 1998 with the ECA 1972. This suggests the student has not read the ECA 1972 or the HRA 1998. The student should have provided evidence in support of his/her argument

Theorists such as Dicey consider Parliament to be supreme. The European Convention on Human Rights now means that Parliament cannot pass any law that is against the Human Rights Act and so this means that Parliament is no longer supreme. However, Parliament was the body that enacted the Human Rights Act and it can repeal the Act and so Parliament is still supreme in the sense that it has only temporarily limited its power.

Correct, although the student could have made a reference to the case of *Thoburn* and the concept of constitutional statutes for added marks. But, the student needed to provide evidence in support of this point. How did the student know that this is true? S/he should have provided a footnote to the academic source

In conclusion, parliamentary sovereignty may exist as Parliament can repeal the ECA 1972 and the HRA 1998, but the power of Parliament to legislate has been limited by joining Europe and the ECHR and therefore Dicey's theory of sovereignty is not totally correct.

> This does sum up the crux of the essay, but it is a little brief. It may have been better to distinguish between the legal reality and the political reality of supremacy and/or to point to the subtleties of the difference between delegation and loss of sovereignty and also the limits of areas covered by EC law and the ECHR. Plus the ECHR is a treaty and not a body. The sentence needed to refer to bodies or documents but not a combination of both

[418 words]

> Overall, this essay attempts to address the question, squarely. There are some serious errors of understanding in relation to the HRA 1998 and how the ECHR operates in the UK. These detract from some of the points that were relatively correct. The paragraph structure needs work so that the essay flows, and each argument is developed and concluded in a single paragraph. Some paragraphs do not end with a conclusion; others do not begin by setting out the point to be made but instead launch into the evidence. Some of the sentences need work to improve their style. There is a lack of evidence to support some of the points being made and a complete lack of references to sources used; this really pulled down the marks to be awarded. The conclusion was a little too brief.

The mark awarded was 45% for a short essay of about 500 words. This essay did attempt to address the subject matter of the question. There was application of some relevant material – reference was made to the EU and the ECA 1972 as well as the HRA 1998. Presentation was adequate; however, the language used was at times formal and at other times informal. The student appeared to be familiar with the subject, although there was some confusion surrounding the Human Rights Act 1998 and the European Convention on Human Rights.

The essay would have been greatly improved by the following:

- an introduction that addressed all the key issues in the title rather than purely sovereignty and the EU;
- a proper series of paragraphs rather than unfinished paragraphs;
- a paragraph defining the main issue in the question – parliamentary sovereignty;
- more evidence to back up the points being made;
- conclusions at the end of each paragraph to round off the issue and to explain its relevance to the question;
- a reference to the text from which the student has taken the example about 'smoking on the streets of Paris';

- a reference to the *Thoburn* case, sometimes known as the *Metric Martyrs* case, rather than purely to the facts of the case. The legal issue in the case needed to be discussed rather than the background facts;
- full case citations and full citations of Acts of Parliament including the year of enactment;
- more formal language;
- proofreading for obvious errors;
- some of the law was correct, but some was muddled – the ECHR and the HRA 1998 were not correctly described.

The essay, if properly written and structured, would probably have achieved a mark in the 50–59% range, although without more evidence to back up the points being made it would have been unlikely to have been awarded a mark of 60% or above.

CHAPTER 2: TEST YOUR KNOWLEDGE OF ESSAY WRITING

It has been suggested that the British Parliament was once supreme, but that its supremacy has been eroded as a result of Britain's membership of the EU and its signature of the European Convention on Human Rights. In order to examine this proposition it is necessary to consider the definition of parliamentary supremacy and differing theories of supremacy. The essay will consider evidence in respect of Britain's membership of the EU and the extent to which that affects Parliamentary supremacy. The essay will also consider Britain's signature of the European Convention on Human Rights in the same light.

There is evidence to suggest that as a result of Britain's membership of the EU, Parliament is no longer supreme. Britain joined the European Community and by passing the European Communities Act 1972, gave effect to EC law within our domestic jurisdiction. Section 2(1) states that 'All such rights, powers, liabilities, obligations and restrictions from time to time created or arising by or under the Treaties … as … are without further enactment to be given legal effect or used in the United Kingdom shall be recognised and available in law, and be enforced…' This primacy of European Community law was evidenced in the case of *R v. Secretary of State for Transport ex p. Factortame (No. 2)* (1991), in which EC law was applied in that case even though this meant that sections of the Merchant Shipping Act 1988 had to be disapplied as they directly contradicted EC law.[1] Parliament had passed the Act subsequent to the

---

1 H. Barnett *Constitutional and Administrative Law* (11th edn, Routledge 2015) p. 137.

European legislation and thus there could be no question that the will of Parliament was to legislate in contravention of Community law. This suggests that Parliamentary supremacy has been eroded, as the courts will not apply British law that contravenes directly applicable EC law.

CHAPTER 6: TEST YOUR UNDERSTANDING OF REFERENCING: EXERCISE ONE – CITING OTHERS' WORK

1 'Under any constitution – whether written or unwritten – there must be a source of ultimate authority: one supreme power over and above all other power in the state.'[2]

2 Barnett highlights Dicey's view that parliamentary sovereignty as one of the organising theories of our constitution and its nature and characteristics provoke debate amongst theoreticians of all descriptions.[3] She considers that international lawyers focus on state sovereignty in international terms, whereas political scientists consider sovereignty in the light of political governance. Lawyers examine sovereignty, perhaps unsurprisingly, from a legal standpoint, identifying the nature of legislative power within the state.[4]

3 'However, Locke concludes that if the people:

> … have set limits to the duration of their legislative, and made this supreme power in any person or assembly only temporary, it is forfeited; upon the forfeiture of their rules, or at the determination of the time set, it reverts to the society, and the people have a right to act as supreme, and continue the legislative in themselves or place it in a new form, or new hands, as they think good.'[5]

Or

'However, Locke concludes that if the people: "… have set limits to the duration of their legislative, and made this supreme power in

---

2 H. Barnett, *Constitutional and Administrative Law* (11th edn, Routledge 2015) p. 116.
3 A.V. Dicey, *Introduction to the Study of the Law of the Constitution* (10th edn, Palgrave Macmillan 1885) p. 39 as cited by H. Barnett *Constitutional and Administrative Law* (11th edn, Routledge 2015) p. 116.
4 H. Barnett, *Constitutional and Administrative Law* (11th edn, Routledge 2015) p. 116
5 Locke, 1977, Book II p. 242 as cited in H. Barnett, *Constitutional and Administrative Law* (11th edn, Routledge 2015) pp. 116–117.

any person or assembly only temporary, it is forfeited; upon the forfeiture of their rules, or at the determination of the time set, it reverts to the society, and the people have a right to act as supreme, and continue the legislative in themselves or place it in a new form, or new hands, as they think good." "[5]

Some points to note for guidance:

- You should not simply put quotation marks round the extracts and consider that to be an appropriate answer. This will not be paraphrasing, but rather a direct quote.
- If you are paraphrasing someone else's words, then try to use your own words as far as possible. It is usually easiest to do this by reading a passage, then putting it to one side, so that you may then summarise the points in your own words, rather than trying to use your own words while still looking at the original text. Please do check to see whether you have simply changed round the word order in a sentence, but otherwise copied Barnett's work.
- The paragraphs should be read and analysed and your paragraph should contain a summary of the key concepts.
- Referencing is difficult if you are referencing someone else's source and they have not included a full citation. There are two schools of thought on this: (1) use the reference that the author put in her own footnote; and (2) look up the full reference and put that in your footnote before the 'as cited in' part of your footnote. Barnett lists full citations in the bibliography at the back of her book, so it has been included in the footnotes here.
- Check that you have fully referenced Barnett's work in footnotes, for both paraphrased and quoted passages.

TEST YOUR UNDERSTANDING OF REFERENCING: EXERCISE TWO – FULL AND ACCURATE REFERENCING

Source 1:

OSCOLA:
Thérèse Murphy, 'Cosmopolitan Feminism: Towards a Critical Reappraisal of the Late Modern British State' in Millns, S and Whitty, N (eds) *Feminist Perspectives on Public Law* (Cavendish Publishing 1999) 19.

Other styles you may see:

Murphy, T, 'Cosmopolitan Feminism: Towards a Critical Reappraisal of the Late Modern British State' in Millns, S and Whitty, N (eds) *Feminist Perspectives on Public Law* (London: Cavendish Publishing, 1999) pp. 19–40.

Or:

Murphy, T, 'Cosmopolitan Feminism: Towards a Critical Reappraisal of the Late Modern British State' in Millns, S and Whitty, N (eds) *Feminist Perspectives on Public Law*, 1999, London: Cavendish Publishing pp. 19–40.

Or:

Murphy, T, (1999) 'Cosmopolitan Feminism: Towards a Critical Reappraisal of the Late Modern British State' in Millns, S and Whitty, N (eds) *Feminist Perspectives on Public Law* London: Cavendish Publishing pp. 19–40.

You may choose to put full stops after the authors' initials and after the abbreviation for pages (p. or pp.) although OSCOLA indicates that this is undesirable.

Source 2:

OSCOLA:
Hilaire Barnett, *Constitutional and Administrative Law* (11th edn, Routledge 2015).

Other styles you may see:

Barnett, H. *Constitutional and Administrative Law* 11th edn (Abingdon: Routledge, 2015).

Or:

Barnett, H *Constitutional and Administrative Law* 11th edn, 2015, Abingdon: Routledge.

Or:

Barnett, H (2008) *Constitutional and Administrative Law* 11th edn (Abingdon: Routledge)

CHAPTER 7: TESTING YOUR UNDERSTANDING OF STYLE ISSUES

1 *'It could be considered that Parliamentary supremacy has been eroded, and some may suggest lost entirely, as a result of Britain joining the European Community.'*

This sentence should be followed with a discussion of the point, including evidence to back up the assertions.

2 '*The <u>Factortame (No. 2)</u> case provided evidence of the way in which European law is interpreted by the domestic courts where there is a conflict between European law and an Act of Parliament. In that instance, the House of Lords granted interim relief to the plaintiffs pending a decision by the European Court of Justice on the meaning and the impact of the European provision. Following the ruling of the European Court of Justice it is clear that in a situation where there is a direct conflict between such an EU provision and an Act of Parliament, the British courts are required to give precedence to the European legislation and, if necessary, to apply this in place of the British Act of Parliament.*'

This sentence would need to be followed with evidence pointing to the relevant judgment within *Factortame (No. 2)*, to back up this assertion.

3 '*It could be suggested that the Human Rights Act 1998 has become semi-entrenched within the British Constitution, if one were to believe that the public would not tolerate any attempt to repeal the Act, and thus that Parliament would not readily repeal the Act.*'

The writer would need to provide evidence to back up this assertion.

BIBLIOGRAPHY

Bradney, A., Cownie, F. and Masson, J. *How to Study Law* (7th rev edn, Sweet and Maxwell, 2014) – Part Two is particularly good on research and on how to read and to use cases and statutes.

Cherkassky, L., Cressey. J., Gale. C., Guth, J., Kapsis, I., Lister, R., Onzivu, W. and Rook, S. *Legal Skills* (Palgrave Macmillan, 2011) – this book combines a wide range of academic and practical skills and with useful advice on legal careers too.

Clinch, P. *Using a Law Library: A Student's Guide to Legal Research Skills* (2nd edn, Blackstone Press, 2001) – getting a little old now, but it is a very good guide to making the most of your library and some research tools.

Dane, J., Thomas, P. and Knowles, J. *Dane and Thomas: How to Use a Law Library* (4th edn, Sweet and Maxwell, 2001) – now a little out of date, but there is some useful guidance to get you started in a law library.

Haigh, R. *Legal English* (4th edn, Routledge, 2015) – very useful as a style guide and should also help with issues of grammar and expression too.

Hanson, S. *Learning Legal Skills and Reasoning* (4th edn, Routledge, 2015) – strong on all aspects of legal method; a particular favourite with students who learn through diagrams.

Higgins, E. and Tatham, L. *Successful Legal Writing* (3rd edn, Sweet and Maxwell, 2015) – another useful text on legal writing.

Holland, J.A. and Webb, J.S. *Learning Legal Rules: A Student's Guide to Legal Method and Legal Reasoning* (8th edn, Oxford University Press, 2013) – particularly good on legal method, on reading the law and on law, fact and language.

Knowles, J. *Effective Legal Research* (3rd rev. edn, Sweet & Maxwell, 2012) – a comprehensive legal research guide that addresses print and online sources, and domestic and EC law.

McVea, H. and Cumper, P. *Exam Skills for Law Students* (2nd edn, Oxford University Press, 2006) – just as the title suggests, this book takes you through exam skills in detail.

Murray, R. *How to Write a Thesis* (2nd edn, McGraw-Hill International, 2006) – a great book for students who are undertaking dissertations or other forms of extended writing.

Powell, D. and Teare. E. *Writing for Law (Palgrave Study Skills)* (1st edn, Palgrave Macmillan, 2010) – this book guides students through the kinds of assessments often set at undergraduate level.

Salter, M. and Mason, J. *Writing Law Dissertations: An Introduction and Guide to the Conduct of Legal Research* (Longman, 2007) – an extended and comprehensive guide to dissertation writing in a legal environment.

Slorach, S., Embley, J., Goodchild, P. and Shephard, C. *Legal Systems and Skill* (2nd edn, Oxford University Press, 2015) – this text combines a wide range of academic and professional legal skills, covered in an innovative way, coupled with the employability agenda.

Slapper, G. and Kelly, D. *Questions and Answers on the English Legal System* (11th edn, Routledge, 2014) – a useful guide to help you with revision for any English legal system exam. It provides excellent examples of essay and problem question answers.

Slapper, G. and Kelly, D. *The English Legal System* (16th edn, Routledge-Cavendish, 2015) – a strong, annually updated textbook that will provide background and evidence in relation to most aspects of the English legal system (ELS). This may be a useful starting point for essays that involved ELS themes. Visit the book's useful companion website, particularly for its Legal Skills Guides on skills including legal writing and mooting.

Strong, S. *How to Write Law Essays and Exams* (4th edn, Oxford University Press, 2014) – this is a more detailed look at legal writing and provides a comprehensive account of the CLEO writing system to assist with essays and exam writing in law.

INDEX